Waste and Consumptio

D1610990

Simonetta Falasca-Zamponi

This book examines the link between waste and consumption through a cultural approach that integrates environmental concerns with reflections on the role that consumption has come to occupy in our contemporary capitalist societies. The problem of global warming is examined to demonstrate the environmental impacts of consumption and our resistance to change the way we live. The mutual relationship between capitalism and consumption is addressed along with early critiques of industrialization that exposed environmental problems. Next, waste is considered as a consequence of consumption and questions are raised about the quantity of waste produced, modes of waste disposal, and risks related to the production of hazardous wastes. Toxic waste and its illegal dumping are examined, along with the problem of abuse of poorer areas and nations when it comes to disposing of toxic material. Health hazards and contaminants in food are discussed. The question of solutions to the problems created by consumption and waste is raised and the claim is advanced that we do not necessarily need to stop being consumers.

Simonetta Falasca-Zamponi is a Professor of Sociology at the University of California, Santa Barbara, where she teaches courses in social theory and cultural analysis. She is the author of *Fascist Spectacle: The Aesthetics of Power in Mussolini's Italy* and of numerous other works on the relationship between politics and culture.

THE SOCIAL ISSUES
COLLECTION™

Framing 21st Century Social Issues

The goal of this new, unique Series is to offer readable, teachable "thinking frames" on today's social problems and social issues by leading scholars. These are available for view on http://routledge.custom gateway.com/routledge-social-issues.html.

For instructors teaching a wide range of courses in the social sciences, the Routledge *Social Issues Collection* now offers the best of both worlds: originally written short texts that provide "overviews" to important social issues *as well as* teachable excerpts from larger works previously published by Routledge and other presses.

As an instructor, click to the website to view the library and decide how to build your custom anthology and which thinking frames to assign. Students can choose to receive the assigned materials in print and/or electronic formats at an affordable price.

Waste and Consumption

Capitalism, the Environment, and the Life of Things

Simonetta Falasca-Zamponi

University of California, Santa Barbara

Routledge
Taylor & Francis Group

NEW YORK AND LONDON

First published 2011
by Routledge
270 Madison Avenue, New York, NY 10016

Simultaneously published in the UK
by Routledge
2 Park Square, Milton Park, Abingdon, Oxon OX14 4RN

Routledge is an imprint of the Taylor & Francis Group, an informa business

© 2011 Taylor & Francis

The right of Simonetta Falasca-Zamponi to be identified as author of this
work has been asserted by her in accordance with sections 77 and 78 of the
Copyright, Designs and Patents Act 1988.

Typeset in Garamond and Gill Sans by EvS Communication Networx, Inc.

Library of Congress Cataloging in Publication Data
Falasca-Zamponi, Simonetta.
Waste and consumption : capitalism, the environment, and the life of things /
Simonetta Falasca-Zamponi.
p. cm. — (Framing 21st century social issues)
1. Consumption (Economics)—Environmental aspects. 2. Waste (Economics)—
Environmental aspects. 3. Climatic changes—Social aspects. 4. Capitalism—
Social aspects. I. Title.
HC79.C6F35 2011
339.4'7—dc22
2010029863

ISBN13: 978-0-415-89210-0 (pbk)
ISBN13: 978-0-203-83427-5 (ebk)

Contents

꩜

Series Foreword

The world in the early 21st century is beset with problems—a troubled economy, global warming, oil spills, religious and national conflict, poverty, HIV, health problems associated with sedentary lifestyles. Virtually no nation is exempt, and everyone, even in affluent countries, feels the impact of these global issues.

Since its inception in the 19th century, sociology has been the academic discipline dedicated to analyzing social problems. It is still so today. Sociologists offer not only diagnoses; they glimpse solutions, which they then offer to policy makers and citizens who work for a better world. Sociology played a major role in the civil rights movement during the 1960s in helping understand us to racial inequalities and prejudice, and it can play a major role today as we grapple with old and new issues.

This series builds on the giants of sociology, such as Weber, Durkheim, Marx, Parsons, Mills. It uses their frames, and newer ones, to focus on particular issues of contemporary concern. These books are about the nuts and bolts of social problems, but they are equally about the frames through which we analyze these problems. It is clear by now that there is no single correct way to view the world, but only paradigms, models, which function as lenses through which we peer. For example, in analyzing oil spills and environmental pollution, we can use a frame that views such outcomes as unfortunate results of a reasonable effort to harvest fossil fuels. "Drill, baby, drill" sometimes involves certain costs as pipelines rupture and oil spews forth. Or we could analyze these environmental crises as inevitable outcomes of our effort to dominate nature in the interest of profit. The first frame would solve oil spills with better environmental protection measures and clean-ups, while the second frame would attempt to prevent them altogether, perhaps shifting away from the use of petroleum and natural gas and toward alternative energies that are "green."

These books introduce various frames such as these for viewing social problems. They also highlight debates between social scientists who frame problems differently. The books suggest solutions, both on the macro and micro levels. That is, they suggest what new policies might entail, and they also identify ways in which people, from the ground level, can work toward a better world, changing themselves and their lives and families and providing models of change for others.

Readers do not need an extensive background in academic sociology to benefit from these books. Each book is student-friendly in that we provide glossaries of terms for the uninitiated that are keyed to bolded terms in the text. Each chapter ends with questions for further thought and discussion. The level of each book is accessible to undergraduate students, even as these books offer sophisticated and innovative analyses.

Simonetta Falasca-Zamponi offers an intriguing study of something many of us take for granted: the waste our consumption produces. Although there is pressure to "go green," few of us really consider the mechanisms of waste that are built into a capitalist economy. Instead, we focus on production and the impact this has on the environment. In her ingenious analysis, Falasca-Zamponi draws attention to the everyday ways in which we waste, and she proposes solutions, including redefining our needs in terms that do not require the consumption of durable commodities that involve waste. Many of us have learned to recycle, but what if we didn't need to recycle the packaging in which our toys are wrapped because we didn't need our toys after all?

Preface

This book examines the link between waste and consumption through a cultural approach. It integrates environmental concerns with larger intellectual questions on the role that consumption, as a way of life, has come to occupy in our contemporary capitalist societies. Throughout, the book seeks to problematize what it means to waste.

The problem of waste has emerged as one of the most contentious and dramatic consequences of market-driven economic development. Little attention is, however, paid to the reasons why so much refuse is created and why we consume. In this book, I focus on the direct relationship of waste to consumption patterns and life choices. I emphasize the daily degradation that the production of what we discard inflicts on us; from food to dwellings, waste poses hazards to our daily existence.

The book first discusses global warming and contextualizes the relationship between capitalism and consumption. I then look at the historical development of consumption and the immense production of waste that results from both the manufacturing process of a commodity and its use. I address questions about the quantity of waste produced, modes of waste disposal, and risks related to the generation of hazardous wastes. I also examine toxic waste and illegal dumping, and the social issues raised by the unequal geographical distribution of hazardous waste disposal.

In subsequent sections, I reconsider consumption from the point of view of its ability to stand as a form of opposition to rules and authoritarian regimes. I emphasize non-materialistic uses of consumption and propose Bataille's theory of expenditure as an alternative to our current consumption patterns. The book's ultimate goal is for us to become more aware of our impact on the world, to take more responsibility for the decisions we make, and to recognize that what we do has consequences.

1:   Global Warming, Consumption, and Our Way of Life

～～✻～～

Setting the Stage: The Debate on Global Warming

One of the most contentious issues of our time being debated by scientists and the general public at large is the spiraling rise of global temperatures and their potentially destructive effect on our planet. A significant measure in the overall assessment of **climate change** (other measures being precipitation and wind patterns), **global warming** has been recorded as escalating dramatically, threatening to upset the delicate balance of our **ecosystems** at an accelerating rate. Data show that over the last 50 years temperatures across the globe have risen at a rate almost double the last 100 years with the eight warmest years on record all taking place since 1998. Global average temperatures are now projected to rise from three to seven degrees Fahrenheit by 2100 (EPA n.d. b), with expected impacts on the rising sea level, further decline in the summer arctic sea ice, and increased frequency of extreme weather events, in particular tropical storms. The specific environmental and health effects of these drastic changes are hard to predict as they will differ among regions of the world, but we can expect that in the process several animal species will become extinct and the diversity of Earth's ecosystems will be greatly reduced.

Although climate changes have been constant occurrences in Earth's history due to natural causes such as volcanic activities and shifts in the sun's intensity, in the last 100 years human-made causes have increased the amount of heat-trapping **greenhouse gases** released in the atmosphere. In particular, emissions of **carbon dioxide** from burning fossil fuels have escalated and, coupled with deforestation, have generated the rapid rise in temperatures that are disrupting the Earth's equilibrium to an extent never experienced before. These hotter temperatures are prompting governments and world agencies to develop plans for containing predicted damages in the form of heatwaves, flooding, and other natural disasters.

Heat is not in principle a harmful element to humans, animals, and plants. Life on Earth would not be possible without the beneficial effects of greenhouse gases and their warming action. Excessive heat, however, especially at the escalating rates we are witnessing, can cause a chain of reactions, such as the melting of glaciers and rising sea levels, which will hamper ecosystems' natural ability to respond and adapt to climate changes and their effects.

The scientific community, surprised by data from long-term studies, warns about the urgency of the problem and the need to take action in order to decelerate the current transformation. For many people among the lay public and experts alike, however, there is no such thing as global warming. Climate skeptics' websites and blogs aggressively denounce science and call global warming a myth, even though they never explain why scientists would want to create such a myth (Bailey 1993, 2002). According to these "skeptics," scientists are only telling lies and making up stories about melting glaciers and depleting coral reefs; in reality, they claim, there are no crises to contain and no emergency to stop, and therefore—this is their crucial point—no definite need to intervene on the issue of climate change. Other skeptics do not dispute the fact that the Earth is getting warmer, but they contest the scientists' assessment that humans are the principal cause of global warming. Science can only guarantee a 90 percent chance that climate changes are caused by human action, therefore, they claim, we should conclude that human behavior is not affecting the planet and consequently it ought not to be scrutinized and even less modified.

Why a 10 percent possibility of error would stop us from wanting to consider solutions to the threat of global warming is unclear to me. We can however conclude from their claims that detractors of climate change science mainly and fundamentally reject the idea that we should alter the way we live. There is nothing wrong with our way of living, these skeptics suggest, and we should not bear the brunt of wrong predictions. Shame on those who think otherwise!

What is Wrong with Caring About the Planet?

I have always been struck by the vehemence with which some people contest the reality of global warming or make fun of the catastrophic predictions such trend generates. Why is the problem of climate change so polarizing for some, I wonder? Why do some mount a whole crusade to disclaim scientists' projections? And more importantly, even if we were to contemplate the unlikely possibility that there is no global warming, what harm would be caused by reassessing the way we use our planet's resources? Ultimately, what is wrong with caring about the planet?

These questions puzzle me and with this book I hope to make other people ponder about them too. For I believe that, as puzzling as they are, these questions bring to the fore what is at stake in the debate over global warming and climate change; they invite us to reflect on how we think of our place in the world and our relationship to the environment and the future of our progeny. To me, the extreme reactions of the so-called skeptics of climate change, and the venomous nature of their attacks against the scientists who warn about the negative consequences of human activity, reveal that these new crusaders indeed feel harm is being done to something they deeply cherish and care for. They believe they are being threatened by the alarm sounded at global warming. What consequences of taking action on climate change do the skeptics find so upsetting, I ask? What is hiding behind the apparent battle over scientific truth?

This book argues very straightforwardly and a bit provocatively that the crusade against climate change science stands as a defense of consumption: It stands for our right to consume. This right is at the foundation of the market-driven economy promoted by **modern capitalism** and has come to define the way of life in most developed countries. When this way of life is challenged for its destructive effects (since our behavior is precipitating the transformation of Earth and the equilibrium of its ecosystem and would thus need to be modified), it is not surprising that many put up resistance. Our emotions, culture, and economics are invested in the existences we lead and it is hard to change all that we have achieved so far. The question for me is: Are we as individuals in a global community willing to reconsider the way we live in order to avoid Earth's implosion?

We know that the skeptics of global warming are answering this question with a resounding no. They represent the most visible and self-conscious attempt to undermine the legitimacy of climate change advocates and their call for action; but what will the rest of us do? This is really the one million dollar question I pose in this book. For I have taken the skeptics of global warming only as a sort of straw man to start a more general conversation about what we all think should be done to guarantee the survival of future generations. I see this book as an invitation to reflect critically on this issue in the hope of bettering our understanding of what we as a society are willing to do to ensure our future and become more aware of the consequences that our way of living has on the planet. It is my belief that, as a theorist once wrote, we should analyze society "in the light of its used, unused or abused capabilities to improving the human condition" (Marcuse 1964, p. x).

The Argument

Let me now say something more about this book's argument. I have claimed that consumption and our desire to hold on to it are driving the crusade against climate change and I have begun to suggest that our consumption habits are responsible for transformations that are potentially dangerous to our planet. Let me make clear that by pointing to consumption I am not advocating that we should all stop shopping and instead lead ascetic lives in the manner of hermits or monks. Instead, I wish to draw attention to the implications that our life choices carry with them. To this end, I emphasize the connection between consumption and waste—a connection that, I think, most of us care very little about and generally ignore. I want to show that when we defend our right to consume we are also upholding our privilege to create waste. The defense of our right to consume stands as a demand not to be bothered by the consequences of our wasteful behavior. Whether it is fossil fuel, sweatshirts, or disposable coffee cups, we don't want to feel responsible for their life cycle. We don't want to think that all we use is going to end up as waste, garbage, mountains and mountains of unwanted rubbish. But by ignoring these mountains, whether in a real or metaphorical sense, we are actually skirting a huge problem at the heart of our environmental crisis. My main point in this book is to show why this is the case.

In broader sociological terms, this book also takes the debate over climate change as an opportunity to observe the politics of knowledge in action. The conflict over global warming shows us how ideas, beliefs, and values influence the way "truth" is pursued. In the course of the book, this motif of what I will call here "interested knowledge" will reappear especially when we discuss attitudes towards consumption. I think it is important for us all to be aware of what is invested in our claims to knowledge no matter the topic.

I realize that some readers will find my description of this knowledge-making dynamic a bit lopsided since, in the specific case examined here, it seems to target the skeptics of climate change as the ones who let their beliefs affect the way they pursue knowledge. I must say in my defense that I also see scientists who denounce the ills of global warming as being driven by values: In their case, it is in the name of reason and independence from traditions and morals that they advance claims to knowledge. Their belief in the validity of science has its problems too, I believe, and several critics and philosophers have pointed this out. We have no space here for this kind of discussion, and I am just mentioning it so that those who are interested in the sociology of science can explore it further.

But going back to my own knowledge position, there is no doubt that in the debate on global warming I shamelessly support the scientists' approach. I do so, I should add, not in the name of knowledge for knowledge's sake, but because I am concerned about the future of life on Earth. From this point of view, I am more interested in probing the relationship between waste and consumption than in crucifying the detractors of climate change. My ultimate goal is for us to become more aware of our impact on the world, to take more responsibility for the decisions we make, and to recognize that what we do has consequences.

And yet, I do not want to let the global warming skeptics off the hook quite yet! For they have indeed managed to affect the debate on climate change and to undermine the legitimacy of scientists who argue against them. They have succeeded to the point that, according to some polls, the public is becoming ever more doubtful about the reality of global warming and therefore less inclined to act on it. Whether this is true or not we will discuss later. For the moment, I just want to provide a little more background information about the skeptics' position in the debate on global warming. To this end I also want to direct you to their documents and blogs. I encourage you to visit the websites set up by climate change skeptics and to conduct your own exercise in what in sociology we call "content analysis." You should ask: What are the main ideas expressed in these blogs? What do the skeptics argue for and against? Here

I will only give you a taste of it that I find significant as evidence for the argument I stated above; that is, that the skeptics see any attempt to find humans responsible for climate change as a threat to our current economic system (capitalism) and way of life (**consumerism**). Reading their blogs is very instructive for understanding the ideas and fears that guide opposition to climate change science. I highly recommend that you independently engage in this exploration.

Skeptics, Freedom, and the Right to Consume

Before I start my short presentation, let me share the information that energy companies such as Exxon Mobil are financing groups who oppose climate change science. These companies believe that their economic interests are threatened by prospective energy policies that would force them to control their carbon emissions. Oil industries openly admit their fears of the economic consequences that regulating global warming entails and, wishing to protect their market share, support groups that challenge climate science and aim at stopping environmental laws. One of the groups financed by Exxon Mobil, for example, is the **libertarian** think tank Competitive Enterprise Institute. According to the mission statement it provides on its website, the Institute "is a public interest group dedicated to free enterprise and limited government." The statement continues, "We believe that the best solutions come from people making their own choices in a free marketplace, rather than government intervention."

The Institute is part of that group of skeptics we discussed earlier that does not deny the reality of global warming. It is, however, like several other climate change skeptics rabidly critical of any theory claiming that humans cause global warming. It is also strongly opposed to any government intervention that would limit greenhouse gas emissions. In March 1992, the founder of Competitive Enterprise Institute, Fred Smith, clearly stated the Institute's position when he said of global warming: "Most of the indications right now are it looks pretty good. Warmer winters, warmer nights, no effects during the day because of clouding, sounds to me like we're moving to a more benign planet, more rain, richer, easier productivity to agriculture" (Legum 2010).

Smith's idyllic picture of global warming was matched by an equally idyllic description of carbon dioxide in an ad called "Energy" aired under the auspices of the Institute in May 2006. The television commercial praised carbon dioxide as a life-saver. Here is the text of the ad in full:

> There's something in these pictures you can't see. It's essential to life. We breathe it out. Plants breathe it in. It comes from animal life, the oceans, the earth, and the fuels we find in it. It's called carbon dioxide—CO_2. The fuels that produce CO_2 have freed us from a world of back-breaking labor, lighting up our lives, allowing us to create and move the things we need, the people we love. Now some politicians want to label carbon dioxide a pollutant. Imagine if they succeed. What

would our lives be like then? Carbon dioxide. They call it pollution. We call it life.

I should add that in 2002, the Institute published a book by Ronald Bailey, who has recently come to admit the existence of global warming. The book is called *Global Warming and Other Eco-Myths: How the Environmental Movement Uses False Science to Scare Us to Death.*

The Competitive Enterprise Institute's core beliefs and goals are in line with other think tanks and individual skeptics that contest climate science. Similarly to Bailey, they all have come to accept global warming as a reality. Their solution to the problem, however, whatever its causes, is encapsulated in this new mantra word: adaptation. With this notion, the skeptics suggest that there is no need to make any changes to our lifestyle because humans can adapt to new climates. Sterling Burnett, of the think tank National Center for Policy Analysis, put it very straightforwardly in a brief analysis of September 19, 2005: "The growing consensus on climate change policies is that adaptation will protect present and future generations from climate-sensitive risks far more than efforts to restrict CO_2 emissions" (Burnett n.d.). In support of adaptation, Steven F. Hayward of the American Enterprise Institute, another conservative think tank, also stated in an article of May 22, 2006 that one needed to think of alternatives to emissions reductions when it came to policy responses to global warming: "[A] greenhouse-gas-emissions cap ultimately would constrain energy production … A sensible climate policy would emphasize building resilience into our capacity to adapt to climate changes—whether cooling or warming; whether wholly natural, wholly man-made, or somewhere in between" (Hayward 2006).

We can see that even when accepting the existence of global warming, and sometimes even admitting that it is human caused, skeptics hold on tight to their idea that there should not be any interventions in terms of policies aimed at changing our way of living. They advocate maintaining things as they are and staying the course. Their justification for this plan of action is that they resent governmental intrusions and oversight. They make it an issue of freedom and accuse climate change scientists of trying "to impose world government on us and take away American freedom of religion and economy," as one angry skeptic put it (Fogarty n.d.).

Not all climate skeptics are the same, and their approach to global warming varies depending on whether they consider global warming from the point of view of its trend, attribution, and impact. To me, however, one commonality emerges from the diverse arguments the skeptics put forward. And that is: we should not change our economic system. One blogger expressed it very well in this statement: "Beware of how often you play the 'we-do-this-or-we-all-perish' card … How often must we transform and reorganize our entire industrial base, just to avoid a plausible, but somewhat (if not extremely) low probability of leaving ourselves vulnerable to certain slaughter?"

(Global Warming Facts n.d.). We should not have to reorganize our industrial base, the blogger laments.

No doubt, a whole way of life is being challenged by scientists' call for responsibility. Such a call puts in question the wisdom of an economic system whose goal is to produce goods for our unlimited and endless access, our right to spend and consume. To me the skeptics reveal just how hard it is to challenge our reliance on capitalism's expansion and therefore on unlimited consumption, even when we know that a continuous unconditional commitment to this system can turn out to be very perilous.

In the next chapter I will sketch out what I see as the link between capitalism, consumption, and waste, which I have posited at the basis of my argument. I will start by giving a brief account of the mutual relationship between capitalism and consumption as it evolved over time. Do not get me wrong here. I am not trying to launch a moral crusade against the evils of capitalism or to demonize consumption. I just believe that history can help us better understand how we have come to our current predicament. I will then also lay out some early critiques of capitalism and industrialization and will make the argument that such critiques exposed the environmental problems accompanying capitalism at its inception but were unable to articulate the long-term impact of these problems.

DISCUSSION QUESTIONS

1. Do you ever think about the consequences of our way of living on the planet?
2. Do you believe that being more attentive to environmental issues would take away your freedom? What freedoms might be hurt or enhanced by regulations on the emission of greenhouse gases? What is freedom for you?
3. What do you think about the idea introduced here that there is a politics of knowledge?

II: Capitalism and Consumption

The Merriam-Webster dictionary defines consumption as "the utilization of economic goods in the satisfaction of wants or in the process of production resulting chiefly in their destruction, deterioration, or transformation." The first part of this definition specifically highlights two peculiar aspects of consumption. First of all, it refers to consumption in economic terms. By this, I mean that it emphasizes how the goods supposedly being consumed are provided through economic transactions that implicate a producing source other than the subject that consumes. The second aspect implied by this definition is that the consumed goods are intended to satisfy wants or desires, not merely needs. In other words, the definition draws a distinct connection between consumption and capitalism: it is only when a multitude of goods is available to satisfy our fancy, not just our basic needs, that the act of consumption takes place. And capitalism is the economic system which, to this day, has been able to produce commodities at a rate that both quantitatively and qualitatively no other system before it has ever managed to provide.

The historical relationship between capitalism and consumption is no doubt binding, whether we put faith in the Merriam-Webster definition or not, and some scholars point out that there is a reciprocal relationship of influence between the two. What they imply with this claim is that consumption was not created by capitalism or is solely dependent on it, neither was capitalism produced by consumption; rather, the two reinforced each other's happening in the process of their own individual development. A historical review of consumption and capitalism's history illuminates the dynamic relationship that scholars claim unites capitalism and consumption.

In the Beginning ...

Historians place the beginning of modern consumption patterns around the second half of the 17th century in England. At this time, although it involved a very small portion of the population, accumulation of consumer goods became more and more characteristic in the households of town and country dwellers alike. Inventories of the period found in England, as well as in the Low Countries and colonial New England, enumerate a rich list of material possessions that were gradually transforming the interiors of private homes. Among these possessions one could count mirrors, books, and paintings; also curtains, which had practically been absent until then, became ubiquitous by 1700 (de Vries 1993). In addition to household items, clothing appeared to be a priority in the consumption patterns of members of the middle classes.

In general, historians suggest that although the 17th century witnessed an economic decline, consumer demand in this era moved towards increasing material possessions and showed a major shift in how people spent their money. In the case of the Friesian peasants in the Dutch Republic examined by de Vries, for example, pottery substituted for tin and wood bowls, and collections of silver display objects began to make their appearance. Reduced incomes did not seem to stop the peasants from pursuing improvements in material possessions even as they economized in other areas. The same goes for the English professional class of the time studied by Peter Earle (1989), who emphasizes the general upgrading of business classes' domestic interiors as well as clothes. Overall, historians indicate that consumer behavior underwent significant changes in this period, including a rising demand for more and better goods. With a clever play on words, de Vries describes these new patterns of consumption as an "industrious revolution," which supposedly anticipated the **Industrial Revolution**. In the former, decisions made at the household level affected the dynamics of the demand and supply mechanism that regulated the influx of goods on the market. In other words, according to de Vries, consumer taste influenced what was sold on the market. In the case of the Industrial Revolution, thanks to technological innovations and organizational changes, the production of supply assumed a more prominent role. It was responsible for an influx of goods that were offered on the market and that were expected to be absorbed by the public. Factories then provided the opportunities to satisfy people's desires for material goods at a level that had not been possible before.

The escalation of the capitalist **mode of production** no doubt altered people's own understanding of their needs and wants and enlarged their choices. If we follow the historians, however, a desire for goods preceded the actual availability of expendable items. This does not mean that capitalism's rationale was to offer people what they were longing and asking for, and I am not implying that capitalism as a phenomenon is simply the response to a demand for goods. Every economic system is motivated by profits and modern capitalists were not less attracted than others to the venerable profession of money-making. The point to which I wish to draw attention, however, is that desires and consumption fed on each other and that capitalism exponentially multiplied the potential to fulfill both individual desires and consumption while also extending its reach to larger strata of the world population. In the early 20th century, the result of capitalism's power and expansion was **mass consumption**, as we will discuss later. Today, **global capitalism** denotes the scope of capitalism's grip, which is reaching beyond the most industrially advanced countries, and testifies to the presence of a uniform cultural tendency in the world community toward the consumption of goods (Centeno and Cohen 2010). Globalization exposes at its highest degree the interdependence between consumption and capitalism.

Goods, Nature, and Industrial Development

The intensification of labor during the Industrial Revolution due to the lengthening of the working day, the availability of a large pool of workers, and the introduction of machines fueled the industrial production of the 18th and 19th centuries. In particular, the mechanization of cotton spinning facilitated the expansion of the factory system and the growth of urbanization. Large numbers of workers moved to cities around which industries were set up. Manchester, situated in the south-central part of North West England, was one of the world's leading industrialized cities, if not the first. Indeed, Manchester was renamed Cottonopolis in the 19th century in view of its numerous textile factories; Manchester City Council estimates that at its peak in 1853 Manchester had 108 cotton mills.

Industrialization applied scientific knowledge to practical purposes, as is demonstrated by the use of machines and later steam engines in the manufacturing industries. In the wake of the **Enlightenment**, this technical progress was believed to be leading to more wealth and better living conditions for the workers as well as for the rising middle classes composed of business owners and industrialists. In reality, harsh working conditions and long hours, which had been typical of work for men, women, and children in pre-industrial times, continued to be prevalent during the industrial era.

One of the most damning critiques of workers' conditions under industrialism drew right from the case of Manchester. In *The Conditions of the Working Class in 1844*, Friedrich Engels denounced the social misery he saw workers experience in "Cottonopolis," the poverty of their dwellings, the exploitation of women and children in factories, the degradation of the environment. In particular, Engels noticed that the technological innovations that were supposed to ease laborers' conditions in the industries were not achieving that goal. Rather than liberating workers from their toil, machines turned them into their slaves, their appendages. As Karl Marx, with whom Engels collaborated, wrote in his famous work entitled *Capital*, "In manufacture the workmen are part of a living mechanism. In the factory we have a lifeless mechanism independent of the workman, who becomes its mere living appendage" (Tucker 1978 [1972], p. 409).

Marx identified in machines one of the elements that contributed to the exploitation of the worker under capitalism and to the creation of **surplus value** for the industrial owners. Even more pungent than his analysis of class relations, however, was Marx's critique of the output that mechanized work was producing then at a high rate: the world of goods, and especially the relationship of goods to the worker. In the famous discussion of the **fetishism** of commodities in Chapter 1 of *Capital*, Marx warned that under the capitalist mode of production the worker was unable to see the commodity as a product of his/her labor and rather thought of it as having an objective value independent of the human toil that went into it, even their own! More generally,

Marx implied, we think of commodities as "natural" objects, almost as having a life of their own.

Fetishism in some religions indeed refers to the practice of endowing material objects with animated powers. Under capitalism, not only workers' but all human relationships to commodities follow this pattern and we look at the commodity as a self-contained and self-created reality. Furthermore, the relationship between the producer (the worker) and the consumer of the commodity also becomes distorted, Marx warned, as they only relate to the product they create and consume and not to each other. This is because when we use a commodity we forget that somebody made it for us, and we lose the human connection inherent in the commodity.

In broader terms, Marx's analysis of commodity fetishism warned about the impoverishment of human relations one risked when the wealth of societies presented itself as "an immense accumulation of things." Although concerned with the inequality of class structure under capitalism, Marx also alerted us to the effects of capitalism on human nature and social relations.

Of Smokestacks and Coke

Industrialization was such a transformational phenomenon that it attracted a wide array of reactions from social critics and literary figures alike. One example of a response came from the noted writer Charles Dickens. In 1854, he published a novel in weekly installments titled *Hard Times for These Times*. Apparently written to help out the sales of the magazine *Household Works*, where it was featured, the story is considered by critics to be among the least successful of Dickens' works. Set in a fictitious place called Coketown, it dealt with the degradation and inequities that accompanied industrialization in **Victorian England**. Dickens examined the particular case of a manufacturing town where material prosperity was growing rapidly yet was being unmatched by human welfare. As he pointed to disparities in wealth between the middle classes and workers and brought attention to the dismal living conditions of the laborers, Dickens also painted a disconsolate picture of the new landscape created by cotton mills, factories' smokestacks, and dirt-covered houses. As he captured the grimy consequences of industrial production on the living space, Dickens described Coketown as:

> a town of red bricks that would have been red if the smoke and ashes had allowed it;
> but as matters stood it was a town of unnatural red and black like the painted face
> of a savage. It was a town of machinery and tall chimneys, out of which interminable serpents of smoke trailed themselves for ever and ever, and never got uncoiled.
> It had a black canal in it, and a river that ran purple with ill-smelling dye, and vast
> files of buildings full of windows where there was a rattling and a trembling all

day long, and where the piston of the steam-engine worked monotonously up and down, like the head of an elephant in a state of melancholy madness.

(Dickens 1958 [1854], p. 20)

The fictitious name Dickens assigned to the place, Coketown, already encapsulates the town's defining element. For the first part of the town's name, "Coke," did not refer to the American national beverage (which had not even been invented by then). Coke is the solid material residue left from coal baked in airless ovens; it is used as fuel in blast furnaces and smelting ores. Most importantly, coke produces smoke, which Dickens seems to take as the main culprit of the depressing state in which the growing town he so dourly portrays had fallen. It might not be surprising to the reader that the model for Dickens' Coketown was Manchester, the industrial city par excellence we mentioned earlier, where diversified firms grew exponentially during the 19th century and in which capitalism's powerful re-imagining of life went unmatched at this time.

Scars on the natural environment, as those described by Dickens in the passage quoted above, were a common feature of early industrialization. In particular, the **iconic** image of smoking stacks, captured by Dickens' description of Coketown's devastatingly gloomy landscape, vividly represented the new reality of the industrial era. That image did not necessarily have negative connotations. On the contrary, black smoke stood for humans' new capacity to increase commodities' production, including food and clothing. It stood for progress and a rich economy; it also stood for urbanization and population growth. Today, that image reminds us of our dependence on carbon fuels and the impact of energy sources on our planet's ecological balance. Smoking stacks were producing carbon dioxide, which, as we now know, has longer-term consequences on the globe than the mere visual defacement of the landscape portrayed by novelists and artists of the time.

In saying this, I do not mean to criticize artists' early depictions of industrialization. However shortsighted their analyses, intellectuals and artists of the time were nonetheless among the first to raise critiques of industrialism in the late 18th and early 19th centuries, and they effectively focused on the ill consequences of mechanized labor on the workers both inside the factories and in their home dwellings and urban environments. For the **Romantics**, in particular, the new reality and overpowering presence of machines raised spiritual concerns about its effects on humans' relation to nature and, more broadly, on human experience. Machines symbolically represented the fettering of freedom and imagination and epitomized the threat to creativity and art brought about by the triumph of technical knowledge (Williams 1983).

In England, poets such as William Wordsworth and Samuel Taylor Coleridge sang the praises of the senses and avowed their respect and awe for the natural world. At a time when individuals were principally seen as specialized instruments of production and carriers of economic relationships, the Romantics initiated a critique of industrialism's costs on the human spirit. In the footsteps of the Romantics, the writer Thomas Carlyle, who was the first to name "industrialism," glumly described the characteristics of his age in his 1829 essay "Signs of the Times":

> Not the external and physical alone is now mangled by machines, but the internal and spiritual also … The same habit regulates not our mode of action alone, but our modes of thought and feeling. Men are grown mechanical in head and in heart, as well as in hand.
>
> (cited in Williams 1983, p. 73)

The spiritualization of nature implicit in the Romantics' and their followers' negative view of machines represented a reassessment of nature's fate in the industrialized era. Awareness of the environmental degradation that accompanied industrialism remained, however, secondary at this stage of capitalist development. Because the Romantics were concerned with the role of art and the artist in the new epoch of industry and commerce, though, their moral discourse also helped to bring to the fore another important consequence of 19th century economic transformations.

The Romantics' sense of outrage at a world that displaced and downgraded art's special status and regarded art as one among other kinds of production exposed the new reality of market rules. It thus called into question a new figure that was coming to occupy a larger than life position in capitalism's new market relationships: the consumer. Representing the public that the artists supposedly needed to please and satisfy in order to sell their art, the consumer with its buying power emerged as the key protagonist of the capitalist economic system based on **exchange value**. All the commodities that were produced under this system needed to be sold, which means that somebody needed to buy them. Whereas artists feared their creativity could be undermined by the imperative to sell, buyers became the target of an increasingly diversified and quantitatively growing production of goods waiting to be purchased on the market and consumed.

Eventually, capitalism's ability to mass produce gave way to mass consumption, which in Europe boomed in the post-World War II period after having first blossomed in the United States in the early part of the 20th century. It was at this stage that larger classes of people beyond the privileged strata gained easier access to spending. They became part of a consumer public that not only grew at the national level within the most industrialized countries but, as already mentioned, has currently achieved global proportions—periodic crises and financial meltdowns notwithstanding. To refer to this growing spending public in terms of consumer society has become the norm, and consumerism is now regarded as a new ethos, a way of living, a dominant social practice.

Consumerism, Here I Come

An economic and social order based on the endless creation of goods for purchase, consumerism can be equally hailed by supporters and damned by detractors. For the former, it signifies economic well-being and access to a good life, to put it simply. For the latter, consumerism equates personal happiness with the purchase of material possessions; it thus promotes the impoverishment of human spirit. The Merriam-Webster dictionary, striving for a neutral definition, describes consumerism as "the theory that an increasing consumption of goods is economically desirable; *also*: a preoccupation with and an inclination toward the buying of consumer goods." This definition suggests that consumerism implies the economic superiority of a system based on the production of goods. It also presumes, if we want to read into it, that consumerism occurs under conditions in which people are free, if they so desire, to worry simply about purchasing what strikes their fancy. When Eastern Europe was ruled by communist governments, people's inability to obtain a pair of jeans was taken to mean repression and a lack of basic rights in the countries that were part of the Soviet bloc. Conversely, the identification of consumerism with democracy has reached such a point that many equate freedom with freedom to consume. In this scenario, one might say that democracy can be bought by the pound, or the dollar, or the ruble!

Consumerism has indeed democratized access to goods for millions of people the world over, and it is not surprising that capitalism, as the promoter of consumerism, has emerged as a positive influence in the eyes of many due to its openness and inclusiveness. We could say that consumption has sold capitalism to the world! At its current stage, economic globalization, that is, the movement towards the economic integration of different sovereign nations, represents the triumph of capitalist principles. It involves the export from developed economies to less developed ones of financial investments and technologies; it is also based on the idea that the belief in the market and in a way of life based on spending will be shared globally.

Globalization has made possible the capitalist dream of low-cost production, which in its turn ensures the availability of low-price items for sale—a consumer's paradise! We can now buy and own millions of items—"an immense accumulation of things," as Marx observed. The irony is: sooner or later we will toss most of them away. We could not refrain from doing otherwise. Can you imagine yourself surrounded by all the objects you have been given or bought ever since you were born? Think of all the toys and clothes and books, not to talk about bulkier items such as bicycles or beds or even cars that are now filling your memory, if you can still remember all of them! Just to keep the smaller things you would need a very large house, or maybe more than one.

As much as many of us like to consider ourselves as keepers, only selected possessions escape the brutal necessity of our getting rid of stuff. Eventually, we have to come to terms with separating from our possessions, especially the ones we care less for. Garage and yard sales seem to be a good indication of this pattern. (By the way, did you know that there are some people affected by the compulsive need to keep every-thing, including garbage from leftover food and bodily evacuations? This extreme form of obsessive–compulsive disorder is called hoarding and is considered a mental illness.)

The questions we are going to explore in the next chapter address the issue of what happens to all our refuse. Where does it go? What is the life of things after we are done using them?

DISCUSSION QUESTIONS

1. Are you convinced by the Romantics' argument that industrialism and machines alter human nature and transform the way we relate to the natural world?
2. Could you come up with your own definition of what consumption means? Are you a consumer?
3. Do you consider yourself a hoarder, or do you ruthlessly eliminate excess pos-sessions from your life? Which goods have sentimental value for you? Which are there merely to be used and then thrown away?

III: The Production of Waste

According to the charity organization Soles 4 Souls, over 1.5 billion pairs of shoes lay idle in American closets. As hard as it might be to estimate how many pairs of shoes each of us own that we actually wear, and admittedly not all of us have a penchant for footwear, it appears that in 2009 alone American discarded more than 300 million pairs of shoes. This is roughly one pair of shoes for each American, which surely does not sound like much considering all the pairs we still keep in our closets. When we reflect on the sheer numbers involved in our love affair with shoes, however, I, for one, find the amounts quite staggering. I believe they begin to give us a sense of the impact each and every one of us makes on the overall proliferation (and, later, destruction) of goods.

Just a quick look around our houses and apartments can give us a fair approximation of where our passions lie when it comes to shopping. It could be clothes and electronics for some, books or CDs for others, and of course food and beverages of all types. No matter the item, it would be pretty obvious that we like to surround ourselves with possessions of different kinds. Factories and industries would not be able to produce at the high rate they do if we were not avid consumers of all things existing and those yet to come.

Whatever our motivations to buy are, and I am not going to examine them in this book though I recommend you explore this topic on your own, I wish to make one important clarification before we proceed with our discussion. When I talk about shopping and owning I am not particularly referring to extravagant desires and purchases we all have and make every once in a while. Quite the contrary, I am referring to our everyday experiences; most of the activities we are involved in on a regular basis entail the acquisition and employment of objects. Brushing our teeth, buying a drink or lunch, engaging in a sport, attending school, traveling by plane; each and every one of these activities requires the use of material items and, this is the big catch, its eventual disposal. How many toothbrushes will we go through during our lifetime if we follow the rules of good hygiene? More than a hundred for sure! How many Styrofoam cups, disposable bottles, and cans will we employ? And what about tennis balls, pens, and paper or lunch containers that flight attendants are still giving us on intercontinental trips (at least for now)?

Keeping a count might be dazzling, but even more damning, from my point of view, is the thought of where all these things end up. For there is no doubt that, along with consumable objects, we are also producing waste both at the manufacturing stage and at the receiving end. And unless we are compulsive keepers, as I was mentioning earlier, we will need to discard, if nothing else, the wrap with which our food is sold, the oil we use for cooking, the leftovers gone bad. Statistics from 2008 gathered by the **Environmental Protection Agency** (EPA) actually show that in the United States containers and packaging count for the highest percentage of **municipal solid waste** (30.8 percent); food scraps are equivalent to 12.7 percent of the total waste (Municipal Solid Waste 2008).

We all create waste, and you might not be surprised to know that the more we buy, the more we waste (although we did not always waste; see Strasser 1999). Indeed, it appears that the rate at which we waste is a wealth indicator; it grows parallel with the **gross domestic product** (GDP) of a country. When we keep up with the latest technological innovations in cell phones, video games consoles, or television sets, or when we upgrade our automobile models and we follow fashion trends in clothing and apparel, we are both creating waste material and displaying our purchasing power. Think of computers; they have now become a household staple item in rich countries, and since they reach obsolescence within two years of purchase, can you imagine how many of them are going to be disposed of in just a few years, worldwide?

The more we spend the more we dump, even if not necessarily everything we dispense with ends up as waste. According to the United States' Environmental Protection Agency, in 2006 United States residents, businesses, and institutions produced approximately 4.6 pounds of solid waste per person per day. This statistic does not take into account solid waste produced by industrial facilities, which amounts to approximately 7.6 billion tons each year. Although not every country (and especially not the poorer ones) keeps a count of municipal solid waste, and some have differing methodology for assessing measures, evidence shows that wealth produces more waste. Countries' riches, we might say, turn Earth into an enormous dumping site.

The Meaning of Waste

At the beginning of this book, I mentioned that I am interested in understanding what it means to waste. Let's start from scratch by ascertaining what the word means. Etymologically, the word "waste" is linked to the Latin term *vastus*, meaning vast (that's what "waste land" means). Around 1300, however, "waste" came to refer to "useless expenditure" and later in 1400 to "refuse matter" (Online Etymology Dictionary). With this meaning of unusable and unwanted, the term "waste" withstood the wear of time and today still maintains its 1300 definition, as evident from the several synonyms available for it: trash, junk, garbage, rubbish, litter, scrap, etc. Keeping this lineage of meaning in mind, we could say that waste is something that has exhausted its life cycle and that finds itself unemployable for any purpose, a definite refuse. Waste has "no value" and would probably be equivalent to less than zero on a numerical scale. Waste cannot be used and, in addition, it is associated with foul odor and dirt. It evokes images of rotting material and spoilt substances, dead matter and faded life. Waste is something to be avoided; it is a health hazard and a pollutant, and you don't want to touch or smell it (Douglas 1966).

In some countries, the logic that evaluates waste as something useless, valueless, and hazardous, and therefore unwanted is even applied to people, who come to be rejected because they are regarded as garbage, that is, unclean and liable to pollute others. Unable to have social relationships with anybody but their kind, and therefore "unemployable," they are allotted jobs that only deal with refuse. In India, they are aptly called "untouchables."

A wonderful book by Mulk Raj Anand with the same title *Untouchable* (2001 [1935]) vividly portrays what it might feel like to be one of these outcasts. The author recounts one day in the life of Bakha, a sweeper and latrine cleaner, confined to this job by his status in a stratified **caste system** that defines where on a social scale one belongs based on birth. Untouchables, also called Dalit, are so valueless that they are without caste and their polluting danger—increased by being forced to work only with sewers, cadavers, and rubbish—is such that not even their shadow is allowed to be cast over members from the Indian upper classes. On public roads, it is their duty to call out and warn others of their coming, lest they run the risk of contaminating them. In the case of Bakha, he accidentally bumps into a member of the higher caste and therefore becomes guilty of transferring his own impurity onto this person. His day thus takes an unfortunate turn, but what is worse is that no matter the events on any particular day, Bakha will never be able to get rid of his "dirty" status.

According to the French writer Georges Bataille (1985), we identify human activity so much with the processes of production and conservation that anything not geared to these ends, anything that we deem unproductive, becomes meaningless and useless to us. Such is the fate of waste. In principle, waste does not produce anything (although technically it does, as we will see in a moment) and has no **utilitarian** end, unless, that is, we toss stuff away in order to get more stuff. In this way we would maintain what Bataille refers to as "the economic principle of balanced accounts" (p. 118). According to this principle, what we spend is compensated for by what we acquire. This model of productive social activity does not exclude consumption, since without consumption production would come to a stop. It requires, however, that we consume rationally and in a moderate form, Bataille claims. Consumption supposedly needs to be subordinated to production and cannot be connected to unproductive activities such as poetry and theater, or for gambling.

Bataille calls a society based on material utility and production "homogeneous," meaning that all elements in the society are the same and work to be useful to one another so that the productive system can function smoothly. All useless elements are instead excluded from it. Bataille then contrasts social homogeneity to "heterogeneity," which literally means other, different, what is not homogeneous and cannot be assimilated. People who refuse to follow the rule of homogeneous society are heterogeneous, for example, but so is everything that homogeneous society rejects as waste. For Bataille, heterogeneous elements are also recognizable by the fact that they often provoke revulsion. Garbage seen as a disgusting refuse would fit the category of heterogeneity.

Because the heterogeneous world includes everything that results from unproductive spending, Bataille says sacred practices from the realm of religion and magic also belong to the heterogeneous. Think of the activity of praying, for example, the worshipping of images, or the ritual of Holy Communion in Catholicism. These expenditures of effort result in no practical goods, nor in their consumption. What Bataille finds fascinating about sacred things is that they are often surrounded by prohibitions of contact that are supposed to separate them from the profane world, that is, the world of everyday life where people work and produce. Why does Bataille find this fact interesting about the sacred? He notices that other heterogeneous elements are subject to the same rule of isolation as sacred things. Among archaic societies, for example, corpses, as well as relatives of the dead, but also menstruating women, are kept secluded from the rest of the group. They are regarded as dangerous and threatening—a powerful source of contamination that needs to be made inaccessible to the profane world, lest it bring harm to it.

Bataille argues that menstrual blood is treated in the same manner as the sacred, leading him to conclude that what is repulsive paradoxically attains sacredness. This is the case because of what anthropologists refer to as the **duality of the sacred**. According to this notion, the sacred actually takes two forms: it is simultaneously holy and sacrilegious, pure and impure. Within this schema, corpses are impure and unholy, but still belong to the realm of the sacred. Following the same logic, we can see how the qualities of unattractive and disgusting that characterize waste bring it close to sacred things. Waste needs to be isolated and kept separate from our regular daily activities because of its contaminating potential. Waste threatens to pollute us and it is something we desire to avoid.

When we deem something useless, we take our distance from it. Therefore, once we produce waste, we want to forget about it. Out of sight, out of mind, the popular saying goes. But this attempt to forget about it, I would argue, puts us into trouble. On the one hand, it stops us from thinking about the consequences of our wasting habits; on the other hand, it also stops us from paying attention to the huge problems that disposing of waste create. How we get rid of all this impure matter is, excuse the pun, no easy matter.

Landfills and Incinerators

Before we examine the issue of garbage disposal, let's be clear that there are several moments in which wastes are generated: wastes are not just the end result of consumption. They are also involved in the original making of the product—the whole process during which our spending riches are created. As the *Glossary of Statistical Terms* issued by the United Nations reports:

> Wastes refer to materials that are not prime products (that is, products produced for the market) for which the generator has no further use in terms of his/her own purposes of production, transformation or consumption, and of which he/she wants to dispense.

> (United Nations n.d.)

But where exactly are all the things we categorize as waste to go? Where do our garbage riches end up (Rogers 2006; Royte 2005)? In 2008, about 135 million tons of municipal solid waste in the United States was discarded in **landfills** (Municipal Solid Waste 2008): these are selected areas where materials are buried deep in the earth or sometimes just covered with layers of soil. Landfills are Americans' preferred waste treatment method, and the United States only employs **incinerators** for hazardous waste of the kind generated by hospitals. Incinerating is the other main waste treatment method adopted by countries and uses a technology based on the combustion of waste. In contrast to the United States, Europe relies more on incinerators, due especially to the problem of land scarcity there.

Many believe that burning waste has more hazardous consequences than burying garbage, but there are several arguments put forward by detractors and supporters of landfills and incinerators about the advantages and disadvantages of either method. In general, the controversy over which method is better revolves around the environmental effects of the waste treatment in question. Incinerators, for example, are said to have the advantage of eliminating waste but the disadvantage of releasing pollutants in the air through ashes and noxious gases, **dioxin** being one of them. Landfills, on the other hand, avoid air pollution but do not remove waste completely and may pollute water sometimes due to leaks.

I don't know what you think about which method is better. My impression is that there are no perfect ways to get rid of our garbage without incurring environmentally unfriendly side effects. The good news, however, is that the latest technology allows for less pollution and is also able to convert waste disposal processes into providers of partly beneficial outcomes (what I was anticipating earlier when discussing the uselessness of waste). This is particularly evident in Denmark, which, similarly to other Northern European countries, has been more open to relying on incinerators for its garbage management than the United States and the countries of southern Europe (Rosenthal 2010). In 2008, only 4 percent of Denmark's waste was discarded in landfills as compared with 54 percent in the United States. Incineration, instead, counted for 54 percent of Denmark's waste disposal, while in the United States it only amounted to 13 percent. The rest of the waste in both countries was recycled.

Denmark has heavily invested in incinerators with the goal of making them waste-to-energy efficient. This means that Danish incinerators can produce a high rate of energy with the waste they burn. It is not that landfills cannot be used for the same purpose; when waste decomposes in landfills it creates gases, such as **methane**, that can be collected for energy use. However, one ton of waste can create 65 **kilowatt hours** (KWh) of electricity when disposed of in landfills, while when burnt it can generate 590 KWh. On a larger scale, one year's worth of waste could produce eighty million KWh of electricity if burnt—an amount large enough to power seven million homes for one year. If collected from landfills, it would only generate nine million KWh of electricity, enough to power 800,000 homes for one year.

No wonder Denmark is betting on these waste-to-energy plants. From the point of view of a **cost benefit analysis**, incinerators certainly seem to be paying off. What is even better news for us, however, is that by investing on incinerators Denmark has been able to build far cleaner ones than in the past and has therefore managed to decrease the negative effects of incineration on the environment. Thanks to dozens of filters, these Danish state-of-the-art plants can now stop pollutants from being dispersed in the air through their smokestacks. In particular, the filters have even been successful in trapping the super-toxic chemical, dioxin.

Dioxin is part of the so-called "dirty dozen" group of dangerous chemicals that are also known as persistent organic pollutants, and it is one of the most feared **chemical compounds**. It can be emitted in the process of burning waste when not done properly. Dioxin can also result from natural processes such as forest fires and volcanic eruptions, although it is mainly generated as an unwanted result of smelting or of industrial production that utilizes chlorine, such as in paper bleaching or the manufacturing of pesticides. Malfunctioning incinerators, however, are considered the most dangerous source of dioxin release in the environment. If the Danes are successful in controlling this kind of emission in their waste-to-energy plants, they will have achieved results of enormous consequences for the rest of us.

In Copenhagen, Denmark's capital, and in wealthy enclaves outside the city, energy plants that burn household garbage and industrial waste have now become familiar sites. Although a main target of protest in many other places in the world, incinerators stand as a crucial fuel source across Denmark. The Danes have accepted them after being reassured of their clean technology and mindful of their ability to convert trash into electricity. Thanks to incinerators, the country's energy costs have declined and Denmark's dependence on oil and gas has been reduced, too, along with greenhouse gas emissions.

This is a story with a good ending, it would seem. Yet, we need to keep in mind that not all countries or municipalities that use incinerators have obtained the crucial technological advances that safely dispose of toxic waste. In addition, when hazardous materials are produced, accidents can still happen, not to mention the fact that highly concentrated toxic elements always need to be handled separately and cannot be easily disposed. In Denmark, for example, they are shipped to special warehouses where they are kept for countless years. In the next section we will examine the main problems that arise around the production of hazardous waste.

Hazardous Wastes

I was saying above that dioxin is one of the most dangerous **chemical compounds** around (Gallo, 1991). I should add that one of dioxin's most insidious aspects and that contributes dramatically to its potential ill effects is the ability to enter the **food chain**. Because it is fat-soluble, dioxin unfortunately accumulates in fatty tissues of animals, including cattle, chickens, and fish. Through this route, as you can well guess, dioxin also enters the human body. Human exposure to dioxins is indeed principally linked to food, in particular meat and dairy products, where larger amounts of fat are present. Once in the body, dioxins are absorbed by fat tissues and stored for years. It is estimated that dioxins' **half-life** in the human body is between seven and eleven years. The consequences on human health of high levels of dioxin in the body are very serious and can affect several organs, besides the reproductive system. Cancer, developmental problems, and damages to the immune system are among the most severe effects of contamination by dioxin (World Health Organization n.d.).

I also mentioned above that dioxin is mainly the byproduct of industrial processes and, though unwanted as all wastes are, is the necessary outcome of manufacturing practices that are widespread and widely used, such as the chlorine bleaching of paper. This means that chances of potential contamination by dioxins are not negligible. If you visit the World Health Organization website, you will find a list of incidents involving the detection of high levels of dioxins in food. At different times, milk in Germany, pork in Ireland, chicken and eggs in Belgium were all found to contain high levels of dioxins. One particular incident I want to talk about is not, however, connected to food but to the production process. I selected it because it not only shows that accidents happen, but also dramatically demonstrates how easy it is to ignore accidents' devastating potential or deflect attention from their consequences.

It was early in the afternoon on July 11, 1976, when a small chemical manufacturing factory near Seveso in Northern Italy experienced trouble in one of its buildings (Fuller 1979). There, a chemical reaction was being carried out in order to produce trichlorophenol, a particular chemical. But due to different problems during the process, the operation went awry and three thousand kilos of chemicals were accidentally released into the air. Carried southeast by the wind, the toxic cloud contained extremely high levels of dioxins and hovered over an area of 18 square kilometers. It affected several communities in the region and particularly Seveso, from which the accident later took its name.

Having occurred on a weekend when the plant was empty, the accident was not noticed at first. The following day, the company warned local authorities of the aerosol mixture that had escaped, stating that the gases were harmful to agriculture; the population was later advised to avoid eating vegetable products from their gardens. Meanwhile, people and animals living in the area began suffering the effects brought about by the breathing and ingesting of the chemicals. Burn-like skin lesions appeared in children soon after the accident, and small animals, such as rabbits, died in large numbers. The company, however, claimed to be ignorant of the substances that were causing these reactions and failed to notify the communities affected that dioxin might be present in the aerosol mixture. Only on July 20, nine days after the toxic cloud had been enshrouding the area over the surrounding communities, was it officially communicated by the company headquarters that dioxins had been released with the cloud of gases. On July 26, the population was finally evacuated from sections of the contaminated zone. On August 2, more sections of the zone were declared contaminated and children and women were ordered to leave.

The case of Seveso teaches us a few lessons about accidents that involve toxic wastes. First, it shows that failure of the systems for prevention are a reality; second, it suggests that accidents are a normal aspect of operations for industrial systems, and they often happen with no warning during routine operations (Beck 1992; Kasperson and Kasperson 2001; Perrow 1984; Quarantelli 1988; Turner and Pidgeon 1995); third, the response to accidents can be very slow as companies try to manage the crisis in ways that benefit their image rather than the populations involved; fourth, accidents happen without being noticed; fifth, we are often unaware of the possibility that accidents might happen. This is particularly striking in the case of Seveso, where neither the local population nor the authorities previously had any worries about the chemical plant or ever suspected the plant to be a source of risk. The factory had been operating in the area for about 30 years, and yet people had no knowledge about the production processes involved in its operations.

In the end, it is important to realize that there is no such thing as zero risk when we deal with the industrial production of hazardous chemicals. Risks are a normal part of operations for industries. And while the Seveso disaster did not cause dramatic results in terms of lost human lives, it had traumatic effects on the local residents, and to this day it serves as an example of industrial pathologies (Edelstein 1988; Mastroiacovo et al. 1988; Mocarelli et al. 1991). Instead the risks were dreadfully realized, in the Bhopal gas tragedy in India when a leak released a large volume of toxic substances into the atmosphere (De Grazia 1985). The accident occurred at the Union Carbide pesticide plant on December 1984 and caused over 3,000 deaths, according to official estimates; other government sources claim the death toll to be around 15,000 people.

These are striking figures and one cannot but be appalled by the sheer magnitude of these numbers. Yet, what I want to argue is that focusing on the big tragedies might lead us to think that, as dreadful as they are, these events are just accidental and rare. My point is instead that risk from industrial production of toxic material is an ever-present reality, one that we are often unaware of. Now, you might believe that these kinds of events only happen in certain places far and away. But think of how safe everybody felt about British Petroleum's drilling in the Gulf of Mexico before the oil rig's explosion of April 2010! There is so much written on this accident that I will refrain from saying anything more here. Before I end my discussion of Seveso, however, let me talk about the aftermath of the disaster and more specifically the phase of cleaning up that eventually followed the accident. This part of Seveso's story will introduce us to the next issue we will take up about waste, that is, the problem of toxic waste disposal.

The Afterlife of Waste

Six months after the disaster struck Seveso, the work of decontamination, which involved the removal and disposal of toxic material, began. The company responsible for the accident was put in charge of the operation and took several years to free the area of the toxic material. Next, the company needed to dispose of the contaminated materials it had collected. At this time a whole mystery began. The clean-up operation that was supposed to dispose safely of the contaminated chemicals became a scandal of its own, adding insult to the original offense.

In 1982, the barrels containing the hazardous material from Seveso seemed to have been lost and nobody could tell where they had ended up. A firm had been contracted to find a legal and safe disposal for the drums, but on their route to France, all track of the chemical wastes was lost. Rumors began to circulate, and it appeared that the firm had subcontracted the disposal of the material to two other companies. Later, the toxic barrels were found sitting in an unused slaughterhouse in a little French village—they had not been disposed of safely. Eventually, responsibility for safe destruction of the waste was taken over by the chemical plant, which in 1985 communicated that all the barrels with the toxic chemicals had been incinerated in Switzerland. In 1993, however, the German *ARD* TV broadcast of October 15, "*ARD*-exclusiv" revealed that the 41 barrels burnt in Switzerland did not contain the contaminated chemicals. Instead, these had been supposedly diverted to the former East Germany, where 150 tons of dioxin-contaminated materials were found in a dump in Schoenberg (Gambino, Gumpel, and Novelli 1993).

I am not sure there is an ending to the mystery of Seveso's waste, and it is hard to evaluate the accuracy of the stories on its whereabouts. We can guess from this narrative, however, that disposal of toxic waste is not an easy and straightforward operation. Illegal disposal of toxic waste is, indeed, not an uncommon practice. On a small scale, we might just think of what we put in our garbage can and that will end up in gigantic waste landfills. We are warned by municipal authorities, for instance, that we are not supposed to dispose of paints and toxic solvents or batteries that still contain toxic material in our regular garbage. But is everybody really following the rules? And what happens to this "unsafe" garbage we have produced? Although landfills are supposed to be designed to protect the environment from contaminants, the possibility of waste material reaching ground water is not negligible. The risk of water contamination thus might be low but it remains a threat.

The bottom line is this: we may be technologically savvy and able to build safe methods to dispose of solid waste; however, we cannot make all waste safe. Some of the goods we consume during our lifetime are just plain environmental hazards. The manufacturing processes used to fabricate several of the products we use and services we rely on generate extremely toxic chemicals—a necessarily lethal complement to the ever expanding production of commodities aimed at satisfying our needs. **Nuclear waste**, especially the long-lived high-level type, is a case in point.

Although the disposal of such **radioactive waste** deep underground is considered to be safe, one needs only to read even the simplest account of what is entailed by the management of this waste to feel like you are part of a sci-fi horror movie or a futuristic videogame. Information on the sheer numbers involved would suffice to give us shivers. Did you know, for example, that some radioactive elements in nuclear waste have a half life that counts in the million years? And were you aware that the timeframe for dealing with radioactive material ranges from ten thousand to one million years (look at all those zeroes when I put these words into numbers: 10,000 to 1,000,000!)? Enough to makes me have apocalyptic nightmares! Taking care of this waste involves long-term strategies and complex planning, including finding storage locations in stable geologic formations and then digging tunnels deep into the earth.

In Finland, for example, on a little island one hundred miles from the capital Helsinki, engineers are digging a tunnel 1,600 feet deep into bedrock to store highly radioactive used fuel rods from their nuclear reactors (Overbye 2010). The tunnel will be finished ten years from now and is called Onkalo, which in Finnish literally means "hidden" and which, as a filmmaker shooting a documentary on Onkalo put it, is a "place we must remember to forget." In the deep, dark recesses of this tunnel, the radioactive material, stored in copper containers two inches thick, will be resting for at least 100,000 years or 3,000 generations from now. To give you a sense of what this means, consider that the vaults have to be built to last and survive the next ice age, when it is expected that more stress in the form of two miles of ice will be added on top of Finland and, therefore, Onkalo.

The most worrisome scenario for Onkalo, actually, is not whether it will survive nature's cycles, but whether it will be dug up by other humans in the future, be it accidentally or on purpose. A lost treasure in the form of fuel and weapon material, Onkalo might be regarded as a buried chest of riches to be sought after. Its builders are, indeed, confronted with the big dilemma of warning future generations about the existence of Onkalo or avoiding letting it be known that this secret place even exists. After all, an up-and-coming Indiana Jones might be tempted to try his fortune! But what if the canisters are discovered by ill chance? In this worse-case scenario, as a *New York Times* journalist commented, that would be quite a nasty surprise for our descendants! Conversely, the construction team at Onkalo joked, what if their digging uncovered canisters left behind by some other generation? That would be quite a surprising turn of events, no doubt, as much as unlikely.

Currently, there are between 250,000 to 300,000 tons of high-level radioactive waste in the world in the guise of rods that, while having to cool down for years before being ready to be sealed into containers, are waiting for disposal. How many places will we need to build and then forget, I wonder? Just knowing some basic facts about nuclear waste is mind-boggling to me, and I don't think apocalyptic movies about nuclear disasters even approximate the discombobulating reality of the hazards that nuclear wastes present. The final episode of our story of Seveso adds even another layer to this worrisome picture, because once again it makes us aware of the gap between real and ideal. Waste is supposed to be disposed of safely, but it is evident that abuses take place when it comes to getting rid of waste. This will be our next topic of discussion.

DISCUSSION QUESTIONS

1. What does waste mean to you? Do you do any activities to limit your waste?
2. What are some other lessons we can learn from Seveso besides or instead of the ones I list?
3. Do you ever think about what you throw in the garbage and whether it should perhaps be disposed of somewhere else?
4. Do you have a right to throw things away, to buy new fashions, new music, new electronic devices?

IV: Abused Waste

〜〜✕〜〜

We know that in its futuristic dimensions Onkalo is a best-case scenario when it comes to disposing of nuclear waste, at least speaking from our generation's point of view; Onkalo is built to ensure that the radioactive material we have produced is not going to endanger the current population's health. The crude reality, however, is: there are very few Onkalos around, and at the same time we have thousands of tons of radioactive waste to dispose of. Where does this nuclear waste and all other toxic wastes, for that matter, end up? Answering this question will confront us with problems of abuse and exploitative relationships; they are very much part of waste's story as well as its life cycle.

On the North–South Track

We know that waste gets moved around very frequently, from area to area, from country to country, from continent to continent. We also know that this movement sometimes takes place through legal and other times through illegal means (Isenburg 2000). In addition, studies show that historically poorer neighborhoods within a city tend to become the locations for dumps (Melosi 1981; Pellow 2002). On a global scale, less developed countries play the role of poor city neighborhoods; they become the discarding sites of wealthier nations and, what is worse, the targets of covered-up operations (Galli 1987). Once we look at the geography of waste's relocation patterns, we can also see that waste's migration movements often trail the route from North to South, from richer locales to poorer ones, depending on the nature of the refuse and its level of danger (Dufour and Denis 1998). Waste disposal could indeed be taken as a measure of global inequality and dubious exploitative relationships, as well as human callousness (Mpanya 1992).

If we look at Europe, we can track the North–South route of waste disposal going from this continent down to Africa. This journey of waste has been revealed by several scandals in the last 30 years. In the 1980s, for example, it was discovered that ships traveled from Italy to African countries carrying highly toxic waste. In particular, Nigeria was at the center of a waste trade initiated with agreements between businessmen from both countries who relied on illegal means to make profitable deals. Once unearthed, the scandal exposed that 3,500 tons of toxic waste had been dumped in the small town of Koko, causing death and injuries to animals and humans, in addition to contamination of water in lakes and rivers (Liu 1991). In spite of the scandal, Nigeria, as well as other African nations, is still in the news today as a waste destination from developed countries. In April 2010, a ship bound for Nigeria carrying toxic waste from Germany was intercepted at sea (Maritime Bulletin 2010).

The December 2004 Indian Ocean tsunami helped to uncover hundreds of broken barrels of radioactive and other toxic waste off the coast of Somalia. These barrels were being washed ashore by the tsunami's powerful waves and exposed an illegal traffic of hazardous materials dumped at sea with minimal, if any, precautions (BBC News 2005). Investigations by the United Nations Environment Programme later concluded that European firms were using Somalia to discard all kinds of toxic material, causing diseases and grave illnesses for the Somali population. The report also estimated that at the time it cost as little as two dollars and fifty cents per ton to dump hazardous waste in Africa, while it cost up to 250 dollars to carry out this operation in Europe (Mbaria 2005). Africa was being exploited and its communities exposed to serious ailments because it offered a cheap alternative to legal waste disposal.

Money is clearly a big incentive when it comes to decisions about waste both for those who want to get rid of it and those who want to accept it. In developing nations, a market for scavenged goods and scrap metal has been thriving that has allowed an indiscriminate dumping of waste from more developed countries. India, which like other developing countries imports different kinds of wastes, including toxic **e-waste**, just recently experienced a severe case of radiation exposure caused by imported scrap. In particular, one contaminated piece, which was apparently made of an unidentifiable metal, ended up in a scrap metal shop in the outskirts of New Delhi and sent seven people to the hospital gravely ill (Yardley 2010). The episode alerted us to the hazards of scrap yards in India where chronic health problems affect workers at these shops, even though in most cases these occurrences don't make the news.

As it turns out, waste export business is highly lucrative, especially when it involves hazardous material, and ghost companies that dominate the field in the hope of high profits are ready to take advantage of the gap between rich and poor countries. The problem with hidden economic businesses that thrive off illegal dumping, however, is that they not only take advantage of weak areas and territories. They also follow hazardous procedures for disposing of waste, thus creating safety and health risks for the populations living next to the waste sites (Isenburg 2000). Organized crime is one of the shadow organizations deeply involved in waste business and is particularly active in Southern Italy, where it has contributed to the deterioration of the local ecosystems and the destruction of natural resources (Cianciullo and Fontana 1995).

One of organized crime's most irresponsible actions took place in the 1990s in connection with the traffic of radioactive material off the coast of Calabria, Italy. According to the testimonial of an ex-member of the **'ndrangheta**, the organization sank ships with a cargo of toxic waste during a major operation aimed at getting rid of hazardous chemicals. What have come to be known as "ships of poison" are now sitting at the bottom of the Mediterranean Sea (Bocca 2009). Estimates of ships that were involved in this operation vary from 25 to 55. The uncertainty over figures, however, cannot detract from the reality of high levels of arsenic, chrome, and heavy metals found in fish in the area, not to mention drums floating at sea (Leonardi 2009). I should add that according to this 'ndrangheta informant, the 'ndrangheta is also responsible for carrying out all the illegal dumping of waste in Somalia that we just discussed.

Home Sweet Home

In this book I draw many examples for my discussion from Italy. I am Italian and I am always interested in following what happens there. However, I don't want to give you the impression that Italy is the only place in which these things happen; on the contrary. Let's take a look at a place closer to you.

In the United States, reporters exposed the Love Canal disaster in 1978. This tragedy brought to the forefront the problem of reckless disposal of toxic waste (Colten and Skinner 1995; Beck 1979). Originally planned to make possible the growth of a dream community in the early 1900s, the Love Canal was supposed to be built between the upper and lower Niagara Rivers with the hope of generating power for industries and homes in the new model city. The project, named after the man who sponsored it, William Love, came to a halt due to economic and technological problems, and what remained of William Love's dream was just a partial ditch where the canal had originally been planned.

In the 1920s, the canal became a municipal dumpsite for industrial chemicals produced by the company that owned the property. Eventually, the company covered the dumpsite with soil and sold it to the city in the 1950s. Later in the decade, a school and a hundred houses were built over the site. Filled with 22,000 tons of waste from the chemical factory, the pit of the canal was leaking and contaminating air, water, and soil with **carcinogenic** substances. This dangerous situation, however, did not attract much attention until the summer of 1978 when, after a record amount of rain fell over Love Canal, chemicals leaking through the ground came to the surface along with rotting drum containers. According to the *New York Times'* front-page article of August 1, 1978, at least eleven chemical compounds that had percolated upward through the soil after the torrential rains were potential carcinogens.

What I find particularly disturbing about Love Canal, which is considered one of the worst environmental tragedies in the United States, is the catastrophic and ill-conceived idea of building over waste. Unfortunately, it appears that Love Canal is not an isolated case. In his book on the **camorra**'s criminal activities around Naples in Southern Italy, Roberto Saviano (2006) tells the story of lovely houses built over illegal dumpsites that, after filling to capacity, had been turned into residential grounds. Eager to own their own little villas, middle- to lower-middle-class families bought these new constructions, attracted by their cheap prices. Workers, employees, and retirees got their chance to become home-owners and did not seem to mind that their homes were literally erected on garbage.

Curiously, according to Saviano, the so-called bosses of the camorra have also built their large, lavish mansions over fields of refuse, toxic and otherwise. With all their money, you might wonder, why would they want to do that? As perverse as this might sound, I think that in their case it makes some sense: by setting camp on garbage they are, like Uncle Scrooge, sleeping over their own mountains of gold. For in Campania, where Naples is located, organized crime presides over a very lucrative waste business that includes the illegal disposal of toxic material. Garbage is the camorra's source of wealth, a major supply of money. As one **camorrista** waste trafficker proudly put it, comparing himself with King Midas: "As soon as we touch garbage, we turn it into gold" (Saviano 2006, p. 321). I should add that, among its illegal activities, the camorra also unsafely handles and then dumps toxic waste into quarries. It later extracts building material from these quarries to be used for new constructions—homes whose walls will be exhaling all kinds of toxic gases. Homes, sweet homes!

It would seem that people are willing to tolerate some of the inconveniences of living near garbage and do not realize that garbage might be more than a smelly nuisance. In the winter of 2010, for instance, heavy rains in Brazil destroyed the whole neighborhood of Morro do Bumba in Niterói, near Rio de Janeiro. As it turns out, the neighborhood had been built atop a garbage dump layered with compressed refuse and dirt. More than 400 people were buried in the slide that hit the **shantytown** during the downpour (Barrionuevo 2010). To add more misery to an already heavy toll of lost lives, rescue workers in Niterói had to face the threat of becoming contaminated through contact with the decomposing garbage. Who had the guts to search through mountains and mountains of rotting trash?

We live, it seems, over garbage and we even build with garbage. In 2008 news reports warned that toxic waste mixed with cement had been used as material to build schools in Crotone, Italy—another way to get rid of refuse and even make a profit from it (*La Stampa* 2008). The worst part of the news, however, was that recent tests of blood samples of children attending one of the elementary schools built with the toxic mixture revealed high levels of cancer-causing heavy metals.

The sad truth is, besides scarring the landscape and destroying nature, waste and its improper disposal produce disastrous results on human health. A statistically significant incidence of higher cancer rates, for example, has been reported in the area close to the sinking of "poison ships" in Southern Italy, which we discussed earlier. In the case of Love Canal, we know that children attending the school built on the site of the dump were burned by the toxic waste that leaked to the surface. In addition, the people who built their homes around the canal experienced higher than normal rates of stillbirths and miscarriages, as well as babies born with defects.

As much as we want to get rid of rubbish, it seems, to come back to haunt us. In 2009, containers of Indian steel were stopped at a European port after being detected with high radiation levels. The steel had apparently been fabricated by Indian foundries utilizing scrap metal contaminated with a radiation **isotope**, **cobalt 60** (Yardley 2010)—a case of what I would call "recycling toxicity."

Trashy Food

Contaminants in water, soil, and air also enter our system through malfunctioning incinerators and landfills. Contaminants then make their way into the alimentary products humans and animals consume. For example, we know that the Italian camorra recycles industrial sludge into fertilizers for agricultural purposes. In principle, industrial sludge is not necessarily all bad, since it contains nutrients and organic substances. However, sludge also features high dosages of heavy metals that are damaging to both nature and humans. Switzerland long ago banned the practice of using sludge for agricultural purposes. But few other countries followed suit.

It is also true that even when limits and regulations on the use of fertilizers are in place they are rarely observed. Thus, we should not be surprised to know that **chromium** is often found in wheat and that pesticides are present in milk. As the continuous outbreaks of **E-coli** contaminations in the United States also show, the food industry is hard to monitor and like anything else on this globe does not seem able to escape the iron law of profitability.

In Santa Barbara, California, and nearby counties, polluted water runs off fields and contaminates surface streams and groundwater supplies (Welsh 2010). According to the Central Coast regional board, wells contain unsafe levels of nitrate that could cause health problems such as cancer, diabetes, and Alzheimer's and Parkinson's diseases, among others. Although local farmers are contesting these data and argue that most of the contaminants in the water are "legacy pesticides" from the past, nobody doubts the fact that water is polluted. What might be in doubt is, rather, the financial viability of farming operations when strict rules are being called for and enforced. For, again, money is a big issue when we deal with pollution caused by production activities.

In the end, it is evident that toxic substances are not isolated from us as much as we would like to think. A report from the United States President's Cancer Panel just released in 2010 warns that 300 contaminants have been detected in umbilical cord blood of newborn babies (Kristof 2010). "Babies," the report states, "are born pre-polluted." The report also concludes that some kinds of cancer are particularly on the rise in children.

Staggering numbers and alarming news indicate the reality of chemicals entering our system—chemicals that for the most part are unregulated and untested. According to the World Health Organization, in the year 2002 there were 20,000 people who died from air pollution in India, 10,400 in Germany, and 23,800 in Japan (World Health Organization 2002). The main source of human-made air pollution is the combustion of fossil fuels from power plants, factories, and automobiles. Although air pollution also has natural causes and has been experienced as a problem throughout history, **anthropogenic** sources of air pollution have risen dramatically in the last one hundred and fifty years. According to the United States Environmental Protection Agency (EPA n.d. a), today just the mobile sources of air pollutants, that is, cars, airplanes, and boats produce more than half of all air pollution in the United States. As much as we think we can control waste, it often and literally goes up in smoke, from the methane gas that exhales from landfills to the carbon dioxide released by our vehicles. Colorless and odorless, these gases invisibly encircle us and unwaveringly enter our organic system with often lethal consequences. The rate at which we consume—it would seem—is consuming us.

DISCUSSION QUESTIONS

1. Are you worried about contaminants in food or do you think our food is safe?
2. What might be some strategies for containing, limiting, or transforming our waste?
3. Do humans inevitably pollute? Why or why not?
4. What do you think about the proverb, "One's man waste is another man's treasure"?

V: Another Look at Consumption

I n the early modern times, the relationship between consumption and waste was at the center of a debate about healthy bodies. Considering that most people experienced hunger and dearth in those years, it is no surprise that consuming food was regarded as a powerful antidote against diseases and death (Porter 1993). Hearty eating and drinking were believed able to neutralize debilitating elements; red meat and wine, in particular, supposedly exercised healing powers over weak constitutions. Food and drinks' consumption stimulated and energized the body, and as long as the waste disposal mechanism worked and evacuations occurred regularly, it was assumed that a healthy balance could be maintained. Yet, not all consumption was considered healthy, and fears also circulated that excessive consumption could actually bring physical collapse. In the late 17th century, **scurvy**, **scrofula**, and a whole other series of pathologies came to be considered wasting diseases—the result of excess. With symptoms such as weight loss and flaccidity, the "consumptions," as these chronic conditions came to be known, assaulted the body, wasting it away. Granted, smoke from coal was also accused of contributing to wasting diseases along with loss of energy and dissolution of strength. However, the big dilemma remained of how to reconcile health with consumption and wealth with waste. A famous treatise on the pathologies of the time by Doctor George Cheyne, *The English Malady* (1991 [1733]), advised against excess by arguing that it could lead to self-destruction. To maintain a healthy body required a balancing act rather than overindulgence, and Doctor Cheyne encouraged moderation.

Consumption's ill effects and its potential for wasting away remained a topic of debate after the 17th century, as consumer society gradually expanded and opened up its gates to wider strata of the population than just the wealthy. Over time, competing definitions about the meaning of consumption emerged that overshadowed the original debate from the 17th century. Consumption still remained a dilemma for its supporters and detractors, but moral issues became more central to the debate as the effects of consumption on the relationship between individual and society attracted more attention. Was consumption good or bad for people? What did it mean to consume? How did consumption affect the well-being of society? Consumption's link to capitalism, in particular, posed challenging questions that were hard to resolve.

Today, consumption, whether condemned, criticized, or hailed has come to represent a whole way of life, a perspective on the world, a mode of thinking. What was the meaning of consumption to those who preceded us? How did attitudes toward consumption evolve? These are the questions we are going to explore in the following sections. As we go through these matters, I want to encourage the reader to reflect again on the politics of knowledge we mentioned in Chapter I. I believe that the debate on consumption effectively illustrates how the way we define an issue has consequences on the way we understand and act on that issue.

Body and Body Politic

We saw earlier that in early **modernity** consumption was evaluated in relation to the body's health. At this time, the nation too was understood as an organic body, a "body politic." The same concerns addressed to individual physiological health in medical discourse also emerged in discussions over the well-being of a country. What could sustain the health of the body politic, it was asked? As for the answer, prosperity was certainly regarded as vital, since poorer nations proved to be vexed with instability and discontent. Wealth, however, needed to circulate and not remain in the hands of the miser, the argument went. Money was to be invested and industries were to grow and expand. The in-and-out flows of the exchange economy would guarantee the commonwealth through the regularized mechanisms of commerce and trade and the involvement of all members of the social organism in the common good. The body politic should not waste away, it was reasoned (Porter 1993).

Yet, despite all warning mechanisms, fears circulated that excessive wealth could undermine the body functions of the nation in the same way that excessive consumption threatened the individual body. The dilemma of how to maintain a balance preoccupied those in charge of the social body as much as it concerned medical practitioners. Justifications and solutions emerged that strove to salvage the merits of an economic system based on production, while contending with issues of consumption and waste. Thus, as I was mentioning earlier, a moral discourse emerged that advocated restrictions on consumption but never demanded an overhaul of the economic system. This contradictory position has characterized approaches to consumption since the 17th century and shows the critical role played by consumption as an activity used to evaluate the importance and centrality of capitalism. As we will discuss in a moment, critiques of consumption were not meant to undermine the capitalist economic model. Rather, discussions revolved around the best ways to cope with the excessive effects of that model. Consumption, at least a certain interpretation of it, became the target of worries and received the brunt of the criticisms; capitalism, in contrast, remained unchallenged.

The Morality of Capitalism

All religions have very specific perspectives and things to say about wealth and its effects on faith. In particular, all religions are wary of the temptations that wealth in the form of money and goods incites. According to noted scholar Max Weber, however, and as paradoxical as this might sound, modern capitalism was enhanced by a mode of conduct inspired by religious teachings. In his renowned work, *The Protestant Ethic and the Spirit of Capitalism* (2002 [1905]), Weber argued that **Puritan** doctrines, and in particular **Calvinism**, promoted the expansion of capitalism by preaching the importance of methodical work. This result occurred because Calvinism endorsed working not in order to pursue pleasure and satisfy needs but as an end in itself, a defense against temptations, and above all a sign of one's salvation.

In his thorough research on the topic, Weber noted a puzzling pattern: early Puritan capitalists were not accumulating wealth for immediate rewards; they rather saw wealth as fruit of labor in a **calling**. The concept of calling, introduced by the **Reformation**, required individuals to fulfill their duties in worldly affairs, that is, people were supposed to display their faith not by praying or by retiring to a monastic life, but by acting in the world. The Calvinists also believed in **predestination**, which stated that only few individuals are chosen to reach final salvation and that God predetermines who they are. By working, the faithful demonstrated that they believed to be the chosen ones. Laboring was a sign of faith, and since self-discipline and frugality were central values in their religious outlook, what the Calvinists gained from their work had to be continuously reinvested and not dissipated in pleasurable activities. The result was that wealth was being accumulated for its own sake. Thus the formation of capital was favored by an ascetic ethos that severely restricted the consumption of riches and turned all gains into investments.

According to Weber's interpretation, religious values promoted capitalism by preaching ascetic practices that shunned the enjoyment of possessions, attachment to external goods, and the desires of the flesh. As Weber writes, "asceticism … defined the pursuit of riches, if viewed as an *end* in itself, as the peak of reprehensibility. At the same time, it also viewed the acquisition of wealth, when it was the *fruit* of work in a vocational calling, as God's blessing" (2002 [1905], p. 116). Within this context, "conspicuous" consumption was to be avoided. One was not supposed to enjoy possessions or indulge in distractions. Idleness was to be reprimanded; in fact, the most reprehensible waste for the Puritans was the wasting of time—a most serious sin.

As peculiar to the Puritans as Weber's thesis is, it shows us a recurring pattern in terms of attitudes towards capitalism and consumption to this day. First of all, it demonstrates how capitalism comes to be perceived as legitimate through its link to the values of work and productivity. Second, it points out that capitalism gets separated and seen as independent from the activity of consumption, although in modern economies the relationship between the two is very tight. Third, it indicates that through this separation of consumption from capitalism, the activity of consumption turns out to be defined as morally dubious in contrast to the ethical standing of capitalist production.

Weber illustrates the dynamics above, though not in so many words, in his book.

In particular, his findings suggest that, granted, a relentless focus on work was the result of the Protestant ethic and the premise for the success of modern capitalism; however, a moral castigation of consumption also accompanied the early development of capitalist production. And, I would add, such moral outlook functioned as a means of control over people's conduct; it was supposed to regulate all forms of consumption, including sexual activities. The Puritans identified unbridled consumption with temptations, lust, and enjoyment, and they thought consumption necessarily led down a path of sinning.

The Puritans were not alone in following this line of thinking. Since modern capitalism's early development, many believed that consumption constituted a threat; it was an evil force that deviated people from following rules, be they religious or, as we will see in a moment, secular. It was argued that consumption brought degradation, though not necessarily of the environmental kind we are discussing here, but of the human mind and body. It disrupted the internal equilibrium of the person and, what is more consequential, of the social organism too. Consumption was ultimately accused of challenging established order and hierarchies.

This moral discourse on the evil of consumption, which developed along with the growth of consumer goods, is what we are going to focus on next. By so doing, we will extricate another dimension of consumption that we have ignored so far: its radical potential and emancipating role.

The Morality of Consumption

Religious discourse on the morality of consumption, similar to the medical rhetoric of the 17th century we examined earlier, targeted excess as the culprit of people spiraling down the path towards wasting away. Although doctors later ascribed consumptive diseases to nervous maladies rather than to excessive eating or drinking, this heavier emphasis on the mental well-being of individuals still indicted consumption as responsible for pernicious lifestyles that shunned simplicity and frugality. Consumption risked endangering one's equilibrium. The degeneration of consuming desires into pathological forms became a central topic of discussion in Thomas Beddoes' famous 1799 treatise on pulmonary consumption, or tubercolosis. In his treatise, Beddoes complained about what he believed was a lack of care for one's body, and he suggested that such neglect was the effect of obsessing with objects and of following fashions that undermined one's health. According to him, well-being was being sacrificed on the altar of fads and in the name of a narcissistic care of the self. If any excess was the culprit, his argument went, it was an excess of sensibility (Porter 1993).

Although not as concerned with the human body as Beddoes was, the famous sociologist Emile Durkheim also linked modern consuming trends to pathological results. Only, in the case made by Durkheim, the health of the body social rather than of the individual body was at stake. In his study of the division of labor (1997 [1892]), Durkheim charged fevered imaginations fed by consumption as the cause for what he called "**anomic**" behavior—a behavior that distanced individuals from feeling a sense of connection with their social community and also freed them from rules and obligations. For Durkheim, social health was dependent on individual moderation and harmonious balance; both could only be achieved by recognizing the need for limits. This was true for the body as well as for the mind of the modern subject. As Durkheim stated, "there is a normal degree of intensity for all our needs, intellectual and moral as well as physical, which cannot be exceeded" (p. 185). Excess, however defined, brought sorrow not pleasure, Durkheim insisted.

Durkheim was not alone in judging with apprehension the changes that modernity was bringing to the individual's relationship to society. The preoccupation with consumption escalated over time, following what some have called the democratization of luxury, that is, the accessibility to larger strata of the population of items previously only available to the upper classes. At the end of the 19th century and the beginning of the 20th, a whole debate about the morality of consumption took place in Europe and the United States. The debate particularly targeted the lower classes, and more specifically their ability to handle the social and economic changes that were opening up to them, what came to be defined as a "world of dreams." Although, once again, the economic rationale guiding the modern expansion of needs was not necessarily questioned or doubted, issues arose on how to reconcile the proliferation of needs and desires with a whole moral tradition that advised self-discipline (Williams 1982). Many wondered: Was the acquisition of material goods a sign of moral degradation and an enslavement of the spirit? Industrial development and economic progress made this question urgent at a time when more than just a privileged few became able and liable to pursue luxury and superfluities. Social commentators and critics asked: What would be the social effects of such democratization? What would happen to the body social? Consumption was seen as a menace and became feared for its disruptive potential, its ability to upset established limits and divisions, and its threat to the traditional status quo.

What emerged then as the response to the perils of consumption in its more modern form was a call to "manage" consumption. It was argued that this measure would ensure the maintenance of the capitalist economic organization by controlling middle- and working-class people's materialistic tendencies. Capitalism, then, was not given up, but control was supposed to be limiting the deleterious consequences on the social equilibrium of an orientation to consume. The trend towards an approach that would organize and contain consumption was clearly evident in Germany, where between 1900 and 1914 articles and books were published debating whether luxury was harmful or beneficial to the individual and the larger society (Breckman 1990–1991). A century-old attack on luxury that targeted all classes engaging in conspicuous consumption was reignited. The solution critics proposed was to control spending both for the middle classes, which seemed to be losing vitality as they fell prey to **hedonism**, and for the working classes whose inclination to emulate the higher classes, it was suspected, could become a source of class hatred and thus a social disruption.

You can begin to see here that denunciations about an expanding access to goods involved more than a mere morality issue. At stake was a whole system of social order that was hierarchically organized and in which people were expected to remain within their own rank. Demands for equal access to consumption entailed moving up the ladder and challenging economic and social hierarchies; it potentially threatened to exacerbate class conflicts and upset social organization. More than moral values, the hostility against consumption, carried out in the name of traditional and often religious stances, actually stood for a defense of the status quo. Power struggle infused the wealthier classes' negative evaluation of the lower classes' ability to discipline their desires.

This link I am suggesting between the desire for social stability and fear of consumption was very evident in the United States. Robert and Helen Lynd's study of Muncie, Indiana, at the turn of the 20th century constitutes a classical case in point. In their book, *Middletown* (a pseudonym for Muncie), the Lynds (1959 [1929]) denounced the new mass leisure activities available to the people of Middletown for fostering individualism and encouraging the pursuit of personal needs. According to the Lynds, movies, radio, and car rides, differently from book discussion clubs, for instance, promoted self-centered, selfish behavior and undermined moral values especially among the youth. The Lynds accused technological innovations, such as the radio, of turning people into passive users and contributing to loosening community and family ties, and also religious beliefs. Considering that 70 percent of the population in Middletown was working class, we can deduce that the Lynds' fears were particularly directed at the workers and their families, whom they did not trust as able to resist the supposedly ill effects of the new leisure and spending opportunities.

American Progressive reformers, critics, and ministers were indeed worried about the power and attraction of the new leisure ethic on the popular classes, whom they esteemed unable to control their instincts or exercise restraint. Whether or not they were right in their prediction, there is no doubt that as popular entertainment attracted audiences from all walks of life, commercial culture appeared to threaten traditional class divisions, as well as established gender roles and, more generally, conservative values (Horowitz 1985). Thus, while the Lynds attacked the movies for damaging the lives of Middletown's people, in New York City and other major urban centers, theater and nickelodeons at the turn of the 20th century became the favorite pastimes of working-class girls. Women stepped out in the evenings to attend the shows and sported new, more independent and self-reliant ways of behaving (Peiss 1986). Similarly, women and youth subverted old rules and morals in the mushrooming phenomenon of New York City's cabarets in the early 1900s. There, during the so-called "dance craze," original styles of dancing, from waltz to ragtime, allowed more physical proximity between the couple and promoted new openness about sexual relationships (Erenberg 1981).

At this point, it might be fair to ask: Were these youth and working-class people making bad, uneducated choices about their leisure time, as critics maintained, or were their new practices simply too upsetting to those who always had privileged access to consumption? Or put in another way, what was the driving factor behind critiques of leisure pastimes that persuaded the elites of the need to contain expected negative outcomes from the democratization of culture? For we need to keep in mind, attempts to control popular orientations to consumption did not go unheeded. Aware of mass culture's appeal and of the popular classes' need for diversion, critics such as Walter Lippman advocated a "managerial" approach that would guide people's taste for amusements toward what Lippman thought were more edifying models. Lippman's fantasy of a "democratic social engineering" proposed education as the solution. Education delivered by technocratic elites would reverse the evil of mass consumption by channeling people's desires and irrational passions toward better, more wholesome pastimes. Social control was the solution to the negative effects of leisure culture, and critics had no hesitation advocating it (Jackson Lears 1993).

To summarize the critics' perspective, I think we can emphasize three important points that have emerged from the discussion so far. First, moralists and politicians treated consumption as a threat to their own vision of social order, which implied a hierarchical organization based on competence and refinement. Second, they believed that popular entertainments caused the surrender of reason and the release of desires as well as the lowering of good taste. Third, they advocated a refined culture imposed from above by the elites in order to overcome instincts and domesticate the senses of those classes lacking in self-restraint. More generally, I would like to claim that by supporting the superiority of ideals and reason, critics of consumption indicted the material, that is, the body, as the source of disruption to the social order. Their contempt for the "masses" was based on the belief that the "masses" only followed bodily instincts and passions and did not listen to reason (Carey 1990). This means, in my opinion, that critics feared consumption's radical potential as rooted in the power of the body's senses: what people felt "materialistically" through their eyes, hands, ears, nose, mouth pushed them to make demands for rights they were previously denied, even if in this case rights only meant such simple activities as having fun, listening to music, or dancing.

Fun, the Body, and Emancipation

You might think that dancing and listening to music are harmless and normal pastimes that everybody can and does enjoy. Nothing, however, could be further from the truth as **totalitarian** regimes' approach to consumption makes more than evident (but you can also think of the fears parents felt about Elvis and rock and roll).

In fascist Italy, the dictator Mussolini condemned material desires for promoting individualistic principles and endangering spiritual values (Falasca-Zamponi 1997).

In a political system where the individual was supposed to be subordinate to the government, any attempt to satisfy personal needs was perceived as undermining the social equilibrium. The idea of personal happiness was to be eliminated in favor of an ethic of discipline and sacrifice that privileged the interests of the whole over those of the individual. For Mussolini, material values and unlimited desires were the opposite of **fascism**'s ideals, and he believed that consumption, by enticing the body, had the potential to undermine the regime's power grip. This is because, according to him, consumption encouraged people to chase their desires and therefore focus on themselves rather than the government and what political leaders asked them to do. From this point of view, the regime's resolution was quite radical. It believed that it needed to stop more than just the act of consuming; it also needed to stop desires. The body's impulses at the root of consumption constituted a continuous threat—a form of rebellion against the government's strictures and rules. How the fascists were going to stop desires is another matter. Their intent demonstrates they believed in the need to control and tame the body.

In the 1930s, the Fascist Party enforced rules of behaving that were meant to change people's everyday conduct, from physical activities to ways of dressing, writing, and speaking. Such orders included the prohibition of dancing in connection with fascist events and the ban of the handshake as a form of greeting, but they also comprised the obligation to wear the fascist uniform on specific occasions and to exercise in order to become trimmer and show no weakness for eating pleasures. Orders even targeted details about the use of ties when worn with an important piece of the fascist uniform, the black shirt. In general, the regime considered economic austerity and frugal leisure habits a must, and it evaluated people's faithfulness to Mussolini by their willingness to sacrifice their individual will and follow rules. Eventually, they were supposed to go fight wars. As we can well imagine, consumption hardly fits these aims; doesn't consumption by definition imply the satisfaction of personal desires and private pleasures?

No wonder totalitarian regimes took to the extremes fears of consumption and attempted to pursue homogeneity and uniformity in response to consumption's threat. Nazi Germany and Soviet Russia were no less aggressive than the Italian fascists in their rejection of individualism. The same goes for Chairman Mao's China (Feher, Heller, and Markus 1983). Today, an authoritarian regime such as Iran bans most Western and pop music and North Korea has strict rules on leisure time.

It would seem that, according to authoritarian leaders and managerial liberals alike, sensual enjoyment manifested in acts of consumption turns the latter into a radical act. Working-class young women attending the theater in turn-of-the-century New York or youth enjoying banned music in modern-day Iran represent in principle an attack on traditionalism and authoritarianism. Consumption stands as a proclamation of autonomy and one's right to happiness; by consuming, youth reject rules and demand emancipation, be it sexual or political. Within this context, we could say that the desire for jeans that many people had in Soviet Russia before the fall of the authoritarian communist regime was more than a mere expression of individual fancy; it represented a contestation of official rules on ways of dressing and was therefore also a refutation of the Communist Party's right to impose views and decisions over its citizens.

Marx theorized that only after basic needs are satisfied would human nature be able to be realized in full; we will only enjoy eating bread when we are not dying of hunger and do not have to struggle for food every day (Tucker 1978 [1972]). At that point, we will also be able to relish art because we would not have to worry about procuring food. For Marx, the affirmation of what he called "sensuous nature" was a fundamental right that we as humans have lost. He believed that it will only be possible to reinstate sensuous nature in a society that turns its attention back to the needs of the social human being. Such ideal for Marx required the end of private property and the dismantling of the capitalist economic system, because he believed that capitalism had actually worsened human capabilities for authentic pleasures and joys. Whether or not we agree with Marx's diagnosis, and although Marx did not write about consumption, I believe his theory of the centrality of human sensuous nature captures the radical dimension of consumption feared by critics. The body and the senses spell trouble.

Within this context, if we take away the negative meanings early 20th century critics assigned to what is "material," I believe the critics were not terribly misguided when they identified the senses as potential social danger. The difference between moral reformers and a totalitarian regime such as fascism, then, is only in the degree of power they were each able to exercise in order to stop people from following their passions and wants. In terms of their intent, however, they both shared the same desire for control, and they also confronted the same dilemma. For those who perceived the radical potential of consumption were confronted with the predicament of how to limit consumption while keeping the economy going. Managerial liberals, as we saw, resorted to control; as long as people were not let free, the ills of consumption could be contained. In fascist Italy, Mussolini claimed not to be rejecting capitalism but rather its aberrations and pathological manifestations, which for him included the "utopia of unlimited consumption" (Falasca-Zamponi 1997, p. 137). Mussolini, then, condemned consumption but, by identifying it with industrialism and progress, saved capitalism. Capitalism was in and consumption out, no matter how unlikely it was that this separation could actually be sustained in the reality of economic laws of exchange.

DISCUSSION QUESTIONS

1. How important is consuming to you? What possessions and the buying of new possessions are important to your sense of freedom and identity?
2. When you watch television or listen to music, do you consider yourself a passive consumer?
3. What youth activities today make some social critics very worried?

VI: Excess and Waste Revisited

❦

We have seen that, depending on one's values and beliefs, consumption can take different and often conflicting meanings. We have also seen that consumption, although tied to capitalism, is often viewed as separate from it; and we have concluded that such division allows critics to attack people's desire for spending, while refraining from questioning capitalistic practices. Finally, by retracing the critics of consumption's arguments, we have also come to appreciate consumption's radical potential, its role as instigator in contestations against cultural, social, and political restrictions. From being our bête noire, consumption has turned into our hero.

The reader will ask at this point: So, what are we supposed to do? This is all very confusing! On the one hand, we have discussed how consumption creates massive problems of waste and contributes to an accelerated climate change that does not bode well for our planet's future. On the other hand, we have argued that the act of consuming has a liberating effect in that it conflicts with the status quo and fights traditionalism as well as authoritarianism. What, then, can the solution be to the waste problem we have raised in this book? How do we deal with consumption when it comes to waste? Is recycling an answer and, therefore, should we just keep consuming to death, as long as we take care of how we dispose of things? These are tricky questions and the answers to them are just as treacherous.

Is Recycling the Answer?

Let's first deal with the issue of recycling. The idea that recycling would alleviate the problem of waste created by consumption is certainly well founded and if it could lead us to **zero waste**, as some environmental groups advocate, recycling would be a lifesaver. Yet, one should be attentive to the risks lurking behind such an apparently simple solution. What I mean by this warning is that, if recycling gave us "permission" to consume more, its only advantage would be to aggravate the depletion of natural resources while eliminating our guilty feelings over having done harm to the environment.

Whenever we consume, we put into motion a whole range of activities that include the extraction of raw materials and their transformation into finished goods in the production process. Waste is not just a side effect of the individual act of consumption. In order to be consumed and eventually recycled "something" needs to be produced, and to be produced this something will need primary materials that have to be mined from the natural world. Consumption is only the last stage in a series of acts that are all conducive to environmental hazards and liable to generate more waste. What would then be gained by recycling if it just gave us the leeway to keep producing at a higher rate?

Considering how hard it is for people even to participate in curbside collection, there is a definite risk that we will all take recycling as an excuse to splurge. A more balanced approach to recycling might be the one suggested by the Environmental Protection Agency, which sponsors the slogan reduce–reuse–recycle. Within this tripartite model, recycling only constitutes the final act in a process that first emphasizes the importance of "reducing"—where reducing means lowering garbage production, diminishing our impact on the environment, and more generally preventing waste. Recycling only comes third in this waste hierarchy, after one has already worked to reduce the consumption of raw material and energy usage and has put effort into reusing (and I will let you think on your own about what you could reuse).

As you may well imagine, the debate is raging about benefits and disadvantages of the reduce–reuse–recycle formula. Unfortunately, from my point of view, the debate tends to focus on the recycling part and rarely on the "reduce" component. Even worse, although some dispute that recycling helps reduce pollution, supporters and detractors tend to argue over the economics of recycling and clash about the amount of energy-saving recycling allows. Discussion of the economic pros and cons of recycling confirms once more what we have been arguing all along in this book: there is still overwhelming resistance to consider seriously the environmental consequences of our style of living. What we are more interested in is the economic costs of our actions.

By this, I do not mean to imply that it is impossible to have an economically viable green politics (see, for example, Krugman 2010). I only want to emphasize what little attention is paid to the "reduce" part of the slogan above, that is, the part of the recommendation that directly affects the production of consumer goods and encourages limiting it. I should also add that even when the focus is on production, its environmental effects are rarely questioned. Within this context, labor movements are also caught in the dilemma as they rightly fight for workers' better treatment, especially in a globally oriented market that offers so many opportunities for exploitation and malpractice. Concerned with the creation of jobs and better pay, the labor movement has tended in the past to eschew environmental issues unless they immediately affected conditions in the workplace.

A New Era

While things are in continuous movement when it comes to environmental politics, it is evident to me that we have not yet resolved the fundamental issue at the core of our current sustainability predicament. I am referring here to our relationship to consumption. So, we are back to dealing with our original question: How much are we willing to rethink our way of living? And once again I have to admit that there are very few efforts to deal seriously and comprehensively with the implications of our tendency to spend.

It is not that consumption does not have its critics. As we have seen earlier, the morality of spending was intensely debated at the inception of modern mass consumption, even if such debate tended to consider only consumption's disruptive impact on the social order. Later on, in the 1930s and 1940s, critics of mass consumption worried more about what they saw as the regressive implications of consumption, the possibility, that is, that people would fall victims to the passive state encouraged by mass consumption's goals to amuse us and distract us. "Amusing ourselves to death," as a media scholar once wrote (Postman 1985), makes entertainment our priority and leads us to neglect our abilities to be critical and to engage with pressing social problems. The most ferocious exponents of this position, Theodor Adorno and Max Horkheimer (1976), talked about the stupefaction affecting the public of mass-mediated products. Contrary to the moral critics of the early 1900s, and more contemporary ones too, Adorno and Horkheimer saw consumption as hampering emancipation by making people content with their conditions. If there was any reference to waste in their critiques, it was more in the implicit assumption that, enthralled by the **culture industry**, people were wasting their lives, be it in a moral or intellectual sense.

More benign views of the act of consuming (some of which we have not talked about) emphasize its liberating potential and its role as a form of cultural expression through which people construct meanings (see for example Hebdige 1979; Schudson 1991). And yet, this approach also eschews consumption's material dimensions and impact. Cultural critics rarely conceive of energy waste in connection with consumption or identify waste's link to the possibility of an imminent catastrophe hanging over our heads. Whether they realize it or not, their approach makes capitalism's iron law of selling and buying seem inevitable and permanent.

It is true that only in the last few decades has the human impact on the environment been recognized as having unprecedented consequences on our planet. In view of this novel assessment, scientists in 2004 agreed to name a new geological era for Earth with an initial date set two centuries back (Space Daily 2004). Paul Crutzen, a Nobel Prize-winning atmospheric chemist, coined the term "Anthropocene," which literally means human-caused, for this new era. It stands for the recognition that humans' unparalleled impact on Earth's ecosystem (our heavy use of Earth's resources) rivals that of nature (in the form of erosions and volcanic eruptions) to the point that it has provoked geological changes within a very short time span. To give you an idea of the magnitude of this phenomenon, think that the previous era, the Holocene, lasted 10,000 years. The current carbon dioxide content in the atmosphere signals the significant shift in the impact of human-related activities on Earth. We have now become geological agents; this means that what we do severely affects our planet. Some indeed believe that our doom days are not too far away.

What to do then? Are we caught between two terrible alternatives: the dissolution of the human race or an ascetic life of sacrifice? If consumption and waste are really the culprits, are there other options to a nightmarish future with strict controls and no pleasures? In this book, I have sought to provide readers with a basic understanding of what is at stake when we talk about global warming, consumption, capitalism, waste, and more generally our way of life. My intent was to offer tools for a critical reflection on the state of our impact on the planet, and I have refrained from merely denouncing or promoting activities in support of my point of view. I am proud, in a manner of speaking, to have avoided throwing at you the overused case of sports utility vehicles' (SUVs) unreasonable thirst for oil as an egregious example of waste (although I am doing it now, I realize!). And although I have made my position clear on the need to take responsibility for our actions in the world, I hope I have succeeded in giving you food for thought rather than prescriptions on the issues discussed here. This means you should not expect me to provide you with specific solutions or recommendations. It is up to you now to decide what to do with the knowledge you have.

The Consumer is King (and Queen)

I began this book with questions about the debate on global warming, and I expressed a sense of wonderment at the animosity shown by climate change skeptics towards suggestions that our way of living might be growing unsustainable. I have theorized that the skeptics' ambivalence about global warming reflects their apprehensions for rules and regulations. In particular, I have indicated as a recurrent motif of the skeptics' opposition to any kind of climate intervention their fear that enforcing laws on environmental issues would be equal to taking away freedom. For the skeptics, measures to contain climate changes would disrupt our way of life purely and simply. And I concluded that the freedom invoked by the skeptics amounts to no more than the unfettered ability to produce and therefore consume to their heart's content.

Although I avowed my dismay at their stance, I have however come to appreciate the candor with which these libertarians have openly admitted where the fact of the matter falls for them in the battle over climate change. They have shown no hesitation in being upfront about their attachment to capitalism and our way of living, and they have indicated to the rest of us that we are rather the ones who are ducking the issue.

Just recently, I came across the Center for Consumer Freedom, a self-proclaimed nonprofit organization that, as its name suggests, is explicitly dedicated to preserve our freedom to consume. The Center zeroes in directly on the key issues of freedom and consumption and proclaims as its goal to attack all activists who are "eroding our basic freedoms—the freedom to buy what we want, eat what we want, drink what we want" (Centre for Consumer Freedom n.d.). The Center's advocates believe "the consumer is King. And Queen." Although the Center is mostly committed to the defense of the food and drink industry, its emphasis on the right to choose how we live our lives aligns it with the skeptics of climate change. They both candidly oppose any intervention that would undermine our current lifestyle and capitalist economic system, and they seem to suggest that our priority in the world is to be consumers, or better still, free consumers.

As I said earlier in the book, I am not interested in demonizing the skeptics of climate change or the think tanks that hail the freedom to consume, although I must admit they make for very good "straw men". The outstanding question for me is: What are we all doing? What is our response to these issues? For I don't think we can duck the question any more. Consumption is consuming us through an enormous dilapidation of natural resources and an overbearing waste disposal problem that threatens to pollute us at every twist and turn. Garbage and refuse increase along with our wealth and spending habits, and so are the hazards to our health and the risk of Earth's implosion. Maybe the human race is an adaptable species and maybe our ecosystem is flexible too, but we have no guarantee that this is the case. As we enter the Anthropocene era, the responsibility for the future of our children and our children's children falls on us, whether we like it or not. We can choose to ignore this reality or we can act on it by creating or imagining alternatives that allow us to maintain our pursuit of happiness without endangering the life of future generations to come.

So, you will ask, are you really not going to recommend any alternatives to consumption? Are you sure you do not want to give us your final word on it? Let me just say one thing. In this book, I have examined the topic of consumption from several different angles and one valuable aspect that has emerged from the discussion and that I hope has struck a cord with you is that not all consumption is of a material kind or implies possession. Listening to music, dancing, playing games are forms of consumption. As I suggested earlier, I do not mean to imply with this statement that we need to become ascetics and give up worldly pleasures. But, if there is anything I would suggest about ways of rethinking our relationship to consumption, I believe I would want to keep in mind our capacity to enjoy pleasurable activities that do not necessarily involve, or at least they minimize, material ownership.

A Vision of Excess

I have already discussed one thinker who has offered an alternative view of waste, consumption, and capitalism: Georges Bataille. In his theory of expenditure, Bataille (1985, 1989) challenged a utilitarian approach to the economy as based on the rational investment of surplus and the efficient organization of resources. On the one hand, Bataille believed that the economy could not be understood by referring only to strictly economic facts; the economy has repercussions on other fields and should not be analyzed in isolation from other activities. Bataille thus distinguished between a "restricted" economy, which for him referred to traditional economics, and a "general" economy, which he conceived as taking into account not only the financial structure of society, but also its psychological, cultural, and social dimensions. Following Durkheim, Bataille believed we should look at society as a whole, and not as a sum of its constituent parts. (I believe this point is particularly crucial when we think of the consequences of our economic behavior.)

On the other hand, Bataille emphasized the importance of consumption, which he contrasted to production and accumulation. For Bataille, life is a continuous production of energy that needs to expend itself, since all organisms generate more energy than they need to survive. The sun, for example, produces an overabundance of energy that it offers to the Earth. Plants, in their turn, use the sun's energy and create more of their own, which they then employ for survival but also for useless purposes such as making their leaves beautiful.

Bataille did not believe in restraint; he did not preach an ascetic return to a strict economy of necessity. On the contrary, he advocated a useless pursuit of pleasure following the same logic of giving a gift without expecting a return or, as in the example above, the beautification of leaves: there is no use for leaves to be looking gorgeous. For Bataille, giving is fundamental to humanity and one needs to be prodigal and expend in excess, without purposes, in order to maintain this basic human feature.

No doubt, Bataille's theory is quite peculiar and more complex than I can explain here. I believe, however, that as unusual as it might sound, Bataille's theory helps us to review our relationship to consuming and wasting. Why does it help us? As I just illustrated, for Bataille, humans have a natural need to express themselves in useless, pleasurable ways. We cannot just work and produce, Bataille argued, because this would take away from us an essential dimension of what constitutes our humanity. Bataille, however, realized that especially under capitalism, and regrettably, we tend to confuse accumulation with pleasure and we thus become enslaved to the world of things. Bataille then suggested ways to fulfill our humanity, or what he called our emotional needs, that go beyond possessing. Bataille named these other ways "unproductive expenditures" and defined them as all activities that "have no end beyond themselves" (1985, p. 118). Among others, he listed spectacles, arts, luxury, cults, the search for glory, eroticism.

These activities Bataille mentions refer to different kinds of spending than the ones we would normally think of. But, as one scholar of Bataille puts it, they could mean "the difference between the simple meltdown of a civilization and its possible continuation, but on a very different 'scale'" (Stoekl 2007, p. xiv). In this regard, the distinction Bataille's theory posits between expenditure and waste is particularly remarkable: expenditure does not depend on the capitalist economic cycle of production, consumption, and destruction, even as it still maintains the need for spending.

In view of what is happening to our planet, I believe that a new look at how we consume might not be a bad idea. It will entail rethinking what it means to be happy while mindful of not falling prey to control mechanisms that would dictate and organize our lives in the manner of Big Brother. We do not want and should not have to repress our energies. At the same time, and this is a critical point I hope I made clear in this book, we should also be cautious of identifying freedom merely with the ability to buy. We need to distinguish between having the freedom to acquire and possess something and freedom as a broader affirmation of the individual right to pleasure and aesthetic enjoyment.

As we discussed with the example of the Soviet Union, the demand for jeans there had the symbolic power of contesting authoritarian rules and challenging the Soviet citizens' lack of free expression and autonomy. It was not just about the material acquisition of a pair of trousers made with a special kind of blue fabric, although, of course, it was about that too. Personally, I don't think we should settle for a freedom that only allows us to possess. Freedom is about much more than that and failing to recognize freedom's larger meaning would actually affect the moral fabric of a society not just its sustainability.

After the Gulf

At the moment that this book is being written, images from the Gulf of Mexico's spill fill the television screens and newspapers' front pages—a warning and reminder of the consequences of our dependence on fossil fuels. This precious mineral so sought after is literally being wasted in the deepest recesses of the ocean—a blow to the economic logic of accumulation, but also a slap in the face of all of us who take for granted the existence of our natural resources and the enjoyment of simple activities such as eating seafood, sun tanning at the beach, or admiring sea life. And yet, according to the head of the American Petroleum Institute, Jack Gerard, the spill should not make us rethink the way we do things: "Nothing has changed. When we get back to the politics of energy, oil and natural gas are essential to the economy and our way of life" (cited in Gore 2010). The economy and our way of life should not change, he says.

Meanwhile, clean-up crews in the Gulf are collecting a growing mass of oily trash that is being sent to landfills around the area. Local communities are beginning to worry about the toxicity of the material being stored in their landfills, but are being reassured of its safety by British Petroleum leaders. Toxicologists, however, declare it impossible to determine whether hazardous chemicals are still present in the oil waste. Apparently, the most toxic compounds in oil are volatile, which means they tend to disappear once crude oil reaches the ocean surface, but there is no way to ascertain for sure whether the chemicals most dangerous to human health are still present in the waste (Barringer 2010).

In another part of the globe, far away from the Gulf, young children swim in the polluted waters of the Niger Delta estuary in Nigeria. There, big oil spills have been a daily reality for the last 50 years at a rate of 11 million gallons a year, equivalent to the Exxon Valdez spill every year. Pools of black crude float around lifeless swamps where once shrimps and crabs abounded. In other parts of the Delta, fishermen still insist on launching their nets in the dirty brown waters hoping to get some catch. Disasters here are not exceptional but rather a normal occurrence. Surrounded by a devastated environment from which they once gathered their daily food, the local people are surprised by the world's attention to the Gulf spill. The international and American media never covered the disastrous consequences of oil spills on their wetlands region. And yet, the Niger Delta is the source of ten percent of the United States' oil import (Nossiter 2010).

This news from the recent Gulf disaster eerily repeats the story told in this book and once again shows us the challenge of holding on to our way of life as it is. The news again questions the wisdom of our compulsion to consume as it is being tested by a technology gone awry, waste hazards unchecked, ecosystems destroyed and new threats to human health. It also confirms the everyday reality of disasters and the unequal global distribution of such challenges, and once more raises the problem of the moral consequences of economic choices. Finally, this news reminds us that knowledge has interests and that determining even simple facts, such as the toxicity of waste, can sometimes be a trial.

These are all big issues to ponder, no doubt. Yet I believe that becoming knowledgeable about the link between capitalism, consumption, and waste might help us all reassess our goals and find less destructive alternatives to our search for happiness. The human imprint has transformed our world in unprecedented ways and there is no pushing back the advent of the Anthropocene era. Hiding from the ill effects of our actions on the planet would, however, be self-defeating and unwise.

At present, a 2010 poll by Stanford University Professor Jon Krosnick gives us some hope that public skepticism about global warming is not on the rise, in spite of what many claim. The poll shows that a large majority of Americans believe the Earth's temperatures have been warming and they are also convinced that human behavior is responsible for such trend (Krosnick 2010). This is promising news, indeed, and I would like to conclude this sometime somber book with an uplifting, though slightly distorted, version of the slogan from a famous popular culture character. Buzz Lightyear, the fictional character of *Toy Story*, was eager to go on impossible adventures to save his friends and the day, and he often encouraged his companions to reach higher than their status as diminutive animated objects. Not even infinity was the limit to their ambitious voyages. Allow me to invite you to do the same and in a somewhat silly mode cry: "To the future and beyond!"

DISCUSSION QUESTIONS

1. Do you reuse items that you own or that had been previously owned by others? What kinds of things are you more inclined to reuse?
2. Can you think about other examples of the politics of knowledge with which you are more familiar?
3. What other activities might match Bataille's idea of "useless pursuit of pleasure," or giving a gift without expecting a return? Do you engage in any activities that follow Bataille's model?

References

Adorno, Theodor, and Max Horkheimer. 1976. *Dialectic of Enlightenment*. New York: Continuum Books.

Anand, Mulk Raj. 2001 [1935]. *Untouchable*. London: Penguin Books.

Bailey, Ronald. 1993. *ECOSCAM: The False Prophets of Ecological Apocalypse*. New York: St. Martin's Press.

———. 2002. *Global Warming and Other Eco-Myths: How the Environmental Movement Uses False Science to Scare Us to Death*. Roseville, CA: Prima Publishing.

Barringer, Felicity. 2010. "As Mess is Sent to Landfills, Officials Worry About Safety." *New York Times* (June 15), p. A16.

Barrionuevo, Alexi. 2010. "Rescue Work to Save Scores Buried in a Brazil Landslide." *New York Times* (April 9).

Bataille, Georges. 1985. *Visions of Excess: Selected Writings, 1927–1939*. Minneapolis: University of Minnesota Press.

———. 1989. *The Accursed Share*. Vol. 1. New York: Zone Books.

BBC News. 2005. "Waves 'Brought Waste to Somalia.'" March 2. Retrieved August 23, 2010 (http://news.bbc.co.uk/2/hi/africa/4312553.stm).

Beck, Eckardt C. 1979. "The Love Canal Tragedy." *EPA Journal* (January). Retrieved August 23, 2010 (http://www.epa.gov/history/topics/lovecanal/01.htm).

Beck, Ulrich. 1992. *Risk Society: Towards a New Modernity*. London: Sage.

Bocca, Riccardo. 2009. "Complotto sotto il mare." *L'Espresso* (September 17). Retrieved August 23, 2010 (http://espresso.repubblica.it/dettaglio/politici-e-007-dietro-le-navi-dei-veleni/2109748).

Breckman, Warren. 1990–1991. "Disciplining Consumption: The Debate about Luxury in Wilhelmine Germany, 1890–1914." *Journal of Social History* 24: 484–505.

Burnett, Sterling. (n.d.). "Climate Change: Consensus Forming around Adaptation". Retrieved August 23, 2010 (http://www.ncpa.org/pub/ba527/).

Carey, John. 1990. "Revolted by the Masses." *Times Literary Supplement* (January 12–18), pp. 34–6.

Centeno, Miguel, and Joseph Cohen. 2010. *Global Capitalism*. Cambridge: Polity Press.

Center for Consumer Freedom. (n.d.). "About Us: What is the Center for Consumer Freedom?" Retrieved August 19 (http://www.consumerfreedom.com/).

Cheyne, George. 1991 [1733]. *The English Malady; or, A Treatise of Nervous Diseases*. London: Routledge.

Cianciullo, Antonio, and Enrico Fontana. 1995. *Ecomafia. I predoni dell'ambiente.* Roma: Editori Riuniti.

Colten, Craig, and Peter Skinner. 1995. *The Road to Love Canal: Managing Industrial Waste before EPA.* Austin: University of Texas Press.

De Grazia, Alfred. 1985. *A Cloud over Bhopal: Causes, Consequences, and Constructive Solutions.* Columbia, MO: South Asia Books.

De Vries, Jan. 1993. "Between Purchasing Power and the World of Goods: Understanding the Household Economy in Early Modern Europe." Pp. 85–132 in *Consumption and the World of Goods,* eds. John Brewer and Roy Porter. London: Routledge.

Dickens, Charles. 1958 [1854]. *Hard Times for These Times.* New York: Holt, Rinehart and Winston.

Douglas, Mary. 1966. *Purity and Danger: An Analysis of the Concepts of Pollution and Taboo.* London: Routledge and Kegan Paul.

Dufour, Jean-Paul, and Corinne Denis. 1998. "The North's Garbage Goes South: The Third World Fears it Will Become the Global Dump." *World Press Review* 35: 30–2.

Durkheim, Emile. 1997 [1892]. *The Division of Labor in Society.* New York: Free Press.

Earle, Peter. 1989. *The Making of the English Middle Class: Business, Society and Family Life in London, 1660–1730.* Berkeley: University of California Press.

Edelstein, Michael. 1988. *Contaminated Communities: The Social and Psychological Impacts of Residential Toxic Exposure.* Boulder, CO: Westview Press.

EPA. (n.d. a). "Mobile Source Emissions: Past, Present, and Future. Pollutants." Retrieved August 23, 2010 (www.epa.gov).

EPA. (n.d. b). "NSCEP Frequently Asked Questions About Global Warming and Climate Change." Retrieved August 23, 2010 (www.epa.gov).

Erenberg, Lewis. 1981. *Steppin' Out: New York Nightlife and the Transformation of American Culture, 1890–1930.* Chicago: University of Chicago Press.

Falasca-Zamponi, Simonetta. 1997. *Fascist Spectacle: The Aesthetics of Power in Mussolini's Italy.* Berkeley: University of California Press.

Feher, Ferenc, Agnes Heller, and Gyorgy Markus. 1983. *Dictatorship over Needs.* New York: Palgrave Macmillan.

Fogarty, David. (n.d.) "Climate Debate Gets Ugly as World Moves to Curb CO_2." Retrieved August 23, 2010 (http://www.reuters.com/article/idUSTRE63P00A20100426).

Fuller, John G. 1979. *The Poison that Fell from the Sky.* London: Penguin Group.

Galli, Craig D. 1987. "Hazardous Exports to the Third World: The Need to Abolish the Double Standard." *Columbia Journal of Environmental Law* 12: 71–90.

Gallo, Michael (ed.). 1991. Banbury Report 35. *Biological Basis for Risk Assessment of Dioxin and Related Compounds.* Cold Spring Harbor, NY: Cold Spring Harbor Laboratory Press.

Gambino, Michele, Udo Gumpel, and Silverio Novelli 1993. "L' inganno di Seveso. Che cosa c'era nel reattore. Inchiesta/Documenti su una catastrofe." *Avvenimenti* 20: 7–14.

Global Warming Facts. (n.d.). Data and statistics. Retrieved August 23, 2010 (http://www.ecoworld.com/global-warming/global-warming-facts.html).

Gore, Al. 2010. "The Crisis Comes Ashore: Why the Oil Spill Could Change Everything." *New Republic,* June 10, pp. 10–12.

Hayward, Steven F. 2006. "Acclimatizing: How to Think Sensibly, or Ridiculously, about Global Warming." *National Review Online*. Retrieved August 23, 2010 (http://www.aei.org/article/24401).

Hebdige, Dick. 1979. *Subculture: The Meaning of Style*. London: Routledge.

Horowitz, Daniel. 1985. *The Morality of Spending: Attitudes Toward the Consumer Society in America, 1875–1940*. Baltimore: Johns Hopkins University Press.

Isenburg, Teresa. 2000. *Legale-Illegale. Una geografia*. Milano: Punto Rosso.

Jackson Lears, T. J. 1993. "Mass Culture and its Critics." In *Encyclopedia of American Social History*. New York: Scribner.

Kasperson, Jeanne, and Roger Kasperson (eds.). 2001. *Global Environmental Risk*. Tokyo: United Nations University Press.

Kristof, Nicholas D. 2010. "New Alarm Bells About Chemicals and Cancer." *New York Times* (May 6), p. A29.

Krosnick, Jon. 2010. "The Climate Majority." *New York Times* (June 9), 21.

Krugman, Paul. 2010. "Green Economics: How We Can Afford to Tackle Climate Change." *New York Times Magazine* (April 11), pp. 34–49.

La Stampa. 2008. "Crotone, scuole e abitazioni costruite con i rifiuti tossici: 7 persone indagate." *La Stampa* (September 25). Retrieved August 23, 2010 (www.lastampa.it/redazione/cmsSezioni/.../36787girata.asp).

Leonardi, Michael. 2009. "Italy's Secret Ships of Poison." *Counterpunch* (November 4). Retrieved August 23, 2010 (http://www.counterpunch.org/leonardi11042009.html).

Legum, Judd. 2010. "CEI Founder on Global Warming: 'It Looks Pretty Good … We're Moving to a More Benign Planet.'" Retrieved August 18, 2010 (http://thinkprogress.org/2006/05/17/global-warming-looks-good/).

Liu, Sylvia. 1991. "The Koko Incident: Developing International Norms on Transboundary Movement of Hazardous Wastes." *Journal of Natural Resources and Environmental Law* 8: 121–31.

Lynd, Robert, and Helen Lynd. 1959 [1929]. *Middletown: A Study in Modern American Culture*. Orlando: Harcourt Brace and Company.

Marcuse, Herbert. 1964. *One Dimensional Man: Studies in the Ideology of Advanced Industrial Society*. Boston: Beacon.

Maritime Bulletin. 2010. "Nigeria Seizes Vessel with Suspected Toxic Waste." *Maritime Bulletin* (April 17). Retrieved 23 August 2010 (http://www.odin.tc/eng/articles/265-Nigeria-seizes-vessel-with-suspected-toxic-waste.asp).

Mastroiacovo, Pierpaolo, Amedeo Spagnolo, Ernesto Marni, Luigi Meazza, Roberto Bertollini, and Giuseppe Segni. 1988. "Birth Defects in the Seveso Area After TCDD Contamination." *Journal of the American Medical Association* 259: 1668–72.

Mbaria, John. 2005. "Tsunami: East Africa Coastline Exposed to Toxic Waste Dumped in Somalia." *All Africa* (March 24). Retrieved 23 August 2010 (http://earthhopenetwork.net/East_Africa_Coastline_Exposed_Toxic_Waste_Dumped_Somalia.htm).

Melosi, Martin. 1981. *Garbage in the Cities: Refuse Reform and the Environment, 1880–1980*. College Station: Texas A&M University Press.

Mocarelli, Paolo, Alessandro Marocchi, Paolo Brambilla et al. 1991. "Effects of Dioxin Exposure in Humans at Seveso, Italy." In *Biological Basis for Risk Assessment of Dioxin and Related Compounds*, eds. Michael Gallo. Cold Spring Harbor, New York: Cold Spring Harbor Laboratory Press.

Mpanya, Mutombo. 1992. "The Dumping of Toxic Waste in African Countries: A Case of Poverty and Racism." Pp. 204–14 in *Race and the Incidence of Environmental Hazards: A Time for Discourse*, ed. Bunyan Bryant and Paul Mohai. Boulder, CO: Westview Press.

Municipal Solid Waste. 2008. "Municipal Solid Waste Generation, Recycling, and Disposal in the United States: Facts and Figures for 2008." Retrieved August 23, 2010 (http://www.epa.gov/osw/nonhaz/municipal/pubs/msw2008rpt.pdf).

Nossiter, Adam. 2010. "Half a World from the Gulf, A Spill Scourge 5 Decades Old." *New York Times* (June 17), pp. A1 and A18.

Overbye, Dennis. 2010. "Films on Science: Finland's 100,000-Year Plan to Banish Its Nuclear Waste." *New York Times* (May 11), p. D3.

Peiss, Kathy. 1986. *Cheap Amusements: Working Women and Leisure in Turn-of-the-Century New York*. Philadelphia: Temple University Press.

Pellow, David. 2002. *Garbage Wars: The Struggle for Environmental Justice in Chicago*. Cambridge: MIT Press.

Perrow, Charles. 1984. *Normal Accidents: Living with High-Risk Technologies*. New York: Basic Books.

Porter, Roy. 1993. "Consumption: Disease of the Consumer Society?" Pp. 58–81 in *Consumption and the World of Goods*, ed. John Brewer and Roy Porter. London: Routledge.

Postman, Neil. 1985. *Amusing Ourselves to Death: Public Discourse in the Age of Show Business*. New York: Penguin Group.

Quarantelli, Enrico. 1988. "Disaster Crisis Management: A Summary of Research Findings." *Journal of Management Studies* 25: 373–85.

Rogers, Heather. 2006. *Gone Tomorrow: The Hidden Life of Garbage*. New York: New Press.

Rosenthal, Elizabeth. 2010. "Europe Finds Clean Fuel in Trash; U.S. Sits Back." *New York Times* (April 13), pp. A1 and A10.

Royte, Elizabeth. 2005. *Garbage Land: On the Secret Trail of Trash*. New York: Little Brown and Co.

Saviano, Roberto. 2006. *Gomorra*. Milano: Mondadori Editore.

Schudson, Michael. 1991. "Delectable Materialism: Were the Critics of Consumer Culture Wrong All Along?" *American Prospect*, March 21, pp. 26–35.

Space Daily. 2004. "Welcome to the Anthropocene." *Space Daily* (September 6). Retrieved August 19, 2010 (http://www.spacedaily.com/news/climate-04zzv.html).

Stoekl, Allan. 2007. *Bataille's Peak: Energy, Religion, and Postsustainability*. Minneapolis: University of Minnesota Press.

Strasser, Susan. 1999. *Waste and Want: A Social History of Trash*. New York: Holt.

Tucker, Robert C. 1978 [1972]. *The Marx–Engels Reader*. 2nd edition. New York: W. W. Norton and Company.

Turner, Barry, and Nick Pidgeon. 1995. *Man-Made Disasters*. New York: Walter de Gruyter.

United Nations. (n.d.). *Glossary of Statistical Terms*. Retrieved August 23, 2010 (http://stats.oecd.org/glossary).

Weber, Max. 2002 [1905]. *The Protestant Ethic and the Spirit of Capitalism*, edited by Stephen Kalberg. Los Angeles: Roxbury Publishing.

Welsh, Nick. 2010. "Farmers Protest New Ag Water Pollution Rules." *Santa Barbara Independent* (May 13–20), 24 (226), p. 17.

Williams, Raymond. 1983. *Culture and Society: 1780–1950*. New York: Columbia University Press.

Williams, Rosalind. 1982. *Dream Worlds: Mass Consumption in Late Nineteenth-Century France*. Berkeley: University of California Press.

World Health Organization. (n.d.) "Dioxins and their Effects on Human Health." Retrieved August 23, 2010 (http://www.who.int/mediacentre/factsheets/fs225/en/).

World Health Organization. 2002. "Programmes and Projects, Quantifying Environmental Health Impacts, Deaths and DALYs Attributable to Outdoor Air Pollution: Deaths and DALYs Attributable to 3 Environmental Risk Factors." Geneva: World Health Organization.

Yardley, Jim. 2010. "Radiation in Imported Scrap Metal Raises Health Concerns in India." *New York Times* (April 24), p. A4.

Glossary/Index

A
Adorno, Theodor 44
Africa 27–29, 49
air pollution 32
Anand, Mulk Raj 18
anomic: a term used by Durkheim to indicate lack of norms and rules that potentially result from the changing conditions of modern society 37
'Anthropocene' era 44
anthropogenic: caused by humans 32

B
Bailey, Ronald 6
Bataille, Georges 18, 46–47
Beddoes, Thomas 36
Bhopal gas tragedy 23
bodies
    consumption and health of 33, 34, 36–37
    Fascism's need to control 40
body politic, health of 34
body social 36–37
Brazil 30
British Petroleum 24, 48
Burnett, Sterling 6

C
calling: in Protestantism it refers to the inner urge leading the individual to accomplish a task given by God 35
Calvinism: a branch of the Reformed Church initiated by John Calvin whose central belief was predestination to salvation or damnation 35
camorra: a Neapolitan secret society involved in mafia-like criminal activities 29–30, 31

camorrista: a member of the camorra 30

Capital (Marx) 10

capitalism

    see **modern capitalism**

carbon dioxide (CO$_2$): a colorless and odorless gas produced both naturally and by human activities, especially through the burning of fossil fuels 1, 12, 32

    advertisement for 5–6

carcinogenic: describing a substance that causes cancer 29

    toxic waste 22, 28, 29, 30, 31

Carlyle, Thomas 13

caste system: a system of stratification that divides people based on their status at birth 18

Center for Consumer Freedom 45–46

chemical compound: a substance formed by two or more different chemical elements 21

Cheyne, George 33

chromium: hard, shiny metallic element that can at certain levels be toxic and carcinogenic and is often found in abandoned production sites 31

climate change: major changes in the pattern of temperature, wind, rainfall and snow measured over a long period of time and that can be caused by natural and human factors 1

    adaptation to 6

    'Anthropocene' era of 44

    industry interest groups opposing 5–6

climate skeptics 2, 4–7

    and defense of consumption 3, 45–46

    and desire not to change economic system 6–7

    industry interest groups in support of 5–6

    opposing restrictions on freedom 5, 6, 45–46

cobalt 60: man-made radioactive isotope of cobalt 31

Competitive Enterprise Institute 5–6

The Conditions of the Working Class in 1844 (Engels) 10

consumerism: a system based on the orientation to buying goods 13–14

consumption

    alternatives to 42–43, 46–48

    Bataille's 'unproductive expenditures' 46–47

    bodily health and 33, 34, 36–37

    chasing desires through 39–41

    climate skeptics defense of 3, 45–46

    cultural expression through 44

    defining 8

consumption (*continued*)

    as distinct from capitalism 8

    and emancipation 41, 44

    fears over disruption of social order 38–39, 44

    history of modern capitalism and 8–13

    'managing' of middle and lower classes 37–38, 39, 41

    mass leisure activities 38–39, 44

    morality of 36–39

    and morality of capitalism 34–36

    Puritan attitudes to 35–36

    recurring pattern in attitudes to capitalism and 34, 35–36

    in totalitarian regimes 39–41

    and waste creation 3–4

cost-benefit analysis: an estimate of the benefits and costs of a planned action 21

Crutzen, Paul 44

culture industry: a term coined by Theodor Adorno and Max Horkheimer that refers to the standardized factory-like production of cultural goods, such as movies, novels, and music 44

D

de Vries, Jan 9

Denmark 20–21

Dickens, Charles 11–12

dioxin: a super-toxic chemical known as an organic persistent pollutant 20, 21, 22, 23

duality of the sacred: the idea that the sacred can be both pure and impure 19

dumping of waste 24, 27–30

Durkheim, Emile 36–37

E

E-coli: a common type of bacteria that can make people sick 31

e-waste: waste discarded from electronic equipment and devices 28

Earle, Peter 9

ecosystem: a unit consisting of living organisms and the physical environment, and that is based on a balanced interaction between the two 1

energy companies 5, 23, 48

Engels, Friedrich 10

The English Malady (Cheyne) 33

Enlightenment: a period in Western history and philosophy that emphasized the use of reason 10

Environmental Protection Agency (EPA): an agency of the United States federal government in charge of protecting the environment 17, 32, 43

exchange value: a Marxian term that refers to the value of a commodity sold on the market 13

expenditure, Bataille's theory of 46–47

Exxon Mobil 5

F

fascism: a political ideology and authoritarian form of government founded by Benito Mussolini, who became a dictator in Italy in the 1920s and 1930s 39–41

fertilizers 31

fetishism: the practice of endowing material objects with animated powers in some religions 10–11

Finland 25

food chain: a representation of how nutrients and energy are passed from one living thing to another 22

contaminants in 22, 31–32

fossil fuels 1, 12, 32, 48

freedom

climate skeptics opposition to restrictions on 5, 6, 45–46

confusion with ability to consume 14, 48

G

Gerard, Jack 48

Germany

consumption in Nazi 40

deaths from air pollution 32

dioxins in food chain 22

dumping of toxic waste in East 24

morality of consumption debate in 37–38

relocation of toxic waste to Nigeria 28

global capitalism: a form of capitalism based on the integration of markets across national boundaries and that promotes a uniform cultural tendency in the world community toward the consumption of goods 9

Global Warming and Other Eco-Myths (Bailey) 6

global warming: increase in the average temperature of Earth over time 1–2

Competitive Enterprise Institute on 5

groups opposing 5–6

public skepticism towards 4, 49

globalization 9, 14

greenhouse gases: gases that trap heat in the atmosphere and can be emitted naturally or through human activities 1–2

gross domestic product: measures the total dollar value of all goods and services produced over a specific period of time by a nation 17

Gulf of Mexico oil spill 2010 24, 48

H

half life: the time it takes for a given radioactive isotope to lose half of its radioactivity 22
of dioxins in human body 22
of nuclear waste 25

Hard Times for These Times (Dickens) 11

health
consumption and 33, 34, 36–37
and deaths from air pollution 32
and food contaminants 22, 31–32
hazards of carcinogenic toxic waste 22, 28, 29, 30, 31

hedonism: a doctrine that sees pleasure as the most important human goal 38

heterogeneous society 18–19

hoarding 15

homogenous society 18

Horkheimer, Max 44

I

iconic: refers to a representation that has a recognizable style and has achieved fame 12

incinerator: a furnace that burns waste material 20
Danish development of 20–21

India
Bhopal gas tragedy 23
caste system 18
deaths from air pollution 32
scrap metal 28, 31

Industrial Revolution: a time period beginning in the 18th century in England that was the stage for enormous social, economic, and technological changes, including the mechanization of production systems and the introduction of factory production 9, 10
literary and social criticism of industrialization 11–13

isotope: formed when different atoms from the same element have a different number of neutrons, which in some cases makes them unstable and therefore radioactive 31

Italy
    building over waste 29–30
    fascist 39–40, 41
    fertilizers from industrial sludge 31
    organized crime 28–29, 29–30, 31
    Seveso accident 22–23, 24–25
    'ships of poison' 28–29

J
Japan 32

K
kilowatt hour: a unit of energy that equals the use of 1,000 watts for an hour 21
Koko, Nigeria 27–28
Krosnick, Jon 49

L
landfills: disposal site where waste material is buried 19–21
    building over illegal 29–30
    methane gas in 21, 32
    oil spill waste in 48
    toxic waste in 24, 31, 48
leisure culture 38–39, 44
libertarian: somebody who believes an individual should be free to act without any constraints from the government or the state 5
Lippman, Walter 39
Love Canal 29
Love, William 29
Lynd, Robert and Helen 38

M
Manchester, England 10, 12
Marx, Karl 10–11, 14, 41
mass consumption: the availability of goods for sale on the market to large groups of people 9, 13
methane: colorless, odorless chemical compound and the principal component of natural gas 21, 32
Middletown (Lynd) 38
mode of production: an expression coined by Marx that refers to the specific way in which a society organizes production 9

modern capitalism: a form of capitalism that according to Weber began in the West between the 16th and 17th centuries and that was based on the rational organization of labor and the systematic pursuit of profits, in addition to an orientation to work as an ethical duty 3, 8–11
   consumption's role in evaluating 34
   as distinct from consumption 8
   economic globalization a triumph of 14
   history of consumption and 8–13
   and loss of human sensuous nature 41
   mass production leading to mass consumption 13
   morality of 34–36
   Puritan doctrines promoting 35–36
   recurring pattern in attitudes to consumption and 34, 35–36
modernity: a time period that refers to the industrial era and the move from feudalism to capitalism and the advent of mass democracy 34
Morro do Bumba, Brazil 30
Muncie, Indiana 38
municipal solid waste: trash that is made up of the things we commonly use and then throw away, ranging from food scraps and packaging to old furniture 17, 20
Mussolini, Benito 39–40, 41

N
National Center for Policy Analysis 6
'ndrangheta: a mafia-like criminal organization based in Calabria, Italy 28–29
Niger Delta 49
Nigeria 27–28, 49
nuclear waste: a waste product that contains radioactive material 25–26, 27

O
oil spills 23, 48–49
Onkalo, Finland 25, 27
organized crime 28–29, 29–30, 31

P
pesticides 21, 31
predestination: in some reformed religions it refers to the idea that only a few individuals are chosen to reach final salvation and that God predetermines who they are 35
The Protestant Ethic and the Spirit of Capitalism (Weber) 35

Puritan: member of a Protestant group originally from England that dissented from the Church of England 35
doctrines promoting capitalism 35–36

R
radioactive waste: a waste product that contains radioactive material 25–26, 27
recycling 42–43
reduce–reuse–recycle debate 43
scrap metal in India 28, 31
Reformation: a European Christian movement that wanted to reform the Catholic Church and led to the creation of Protestantism 35
religion
discourse on morality of capitalism 34–36
discourse on morality of consumption 35
sacred practices 19
Romantics: artists and intellectuals belonging to the movement of Romanticism in the 18th century, which strongly reacted against the industrial era and the neglect of nature 12–13

S
sacred practices 19
Santa Barbara, California 31
Saviano, Roberto 29–30
scrofula: infection of the skin on the neck due to tuberculosis 33
scurvy: a disease caused by deficiency of vitamin C and that is characterized by weakness and loss of appetite 33
Seveso, Italy 22–23, 24–25
shantytown: a part of town where poor people live in a slum, often built illegally and mainly consisting of improvised shacks 30
'ships of poison' 28–29
shoes 16
"Signs of the Times" (Carlyle) 13
Somalia 28, 29
Soviet Union 39–40
surplus value: a term used by Marx to indicate the difference between a worker's wages and the value of goods that the workers produce for their boss 10
Switzerland 31

T
theory of expenditure 46–47

totalitarian: refers to an authoritarian form of government based on centralized control in which the individual is subordinated to the state and where the state controls all aspects of people's lives 39

    societies and consumption 39–41

toxic waste 22–23

    Bhopal gas tragedy 23

    building over 29–30

    carcinogenic 22, 28, 29, 30, 31

    illegal dumping of 24, 27–30

    Love Canal disaster 29

    North-South relocation of 27–29

    nuclear waste disposal 25–26, 27

    from oil spills 23, 48–49

    Seveso accident 22–23, 24–25

tsunami 2004 28

U

Union Carbide 23

United States of America

    air pollution 32

    consumption morality debate 38

    food contamination 31

    Gulf of Mexico oil spill 2010 24, 48

    incinerator use 20

    landfills 20

    Love Canal 29

    solid waste statistics 17, 20

    water pollution 31

Untouchable (Anand) 18

untouchables 18

utilitarian: the idea that what is valuable is determined by its utility 46

V

Victorian England: a period in England when Queen Victoria reigned, covering the years from 1837 to 1901 11

    criticisms of industrialism in 11–13

W

waste

    creation and right to consume 3–4

    export business 28

growth in parallel to GDP 17
illegal dumping of 24, 27–30
meaning of 17–19
North-South relocation of 27–29
nuclear 25–26, 27
production of 3–4, 16–17
recycling 42–43
statistics on solid 17, 20
see also toxic waste
wasting diseases 33
water pollution 25, 31
in Nigeria 28, 49
in United States 29, 31
wealth
in the body politic 34
in garbage 30
Puritan doctrine and accumulation of 35
as a waste indicator 17
Weber, Max 35–36

Z
zero waste: a philosophy that aims at reducing and eliminating waste through reuse and recycling and a more balanced approach to consumption 42